THE ENC1

By
BONNIE ROBERTS

Adapted from the novel by
ELIZABETH VON ARNIM

Dramatic Publishing
Woodstock, Illinois • Australia • New Zealand • South Africa

*** NOTICE ***

The amateur and stock acting rights to this work are controlled exclusively by THE DRAMATIC PUBLISHING COMPANY without whose permission in writing no performance of it may be given. Royalty must be paid every time a play is performed whether or not it is presented for profit and whether or not admission is charged. A play is performed any time it is acted before an audience. Current royalty rates, applications and restrictions may be found at our website: www.dramaticpublishing.com, or we may be contacted by mail at: DRAMATIC PUBLISHING COMPANY, 311 Washington St., Woodstock IL 60098.

COPYRIGHT LAW GIVES THE AUTHOR OR THE AUTHOR'S AGENT THE EXCLUSIVE RIGHT TO MAKE COPIES. This law provides authors with a fair return for their creative efforts. Authors earn their living from the royalties they receive from book sales and from the performance of their work. Conscientious observance of copyright law is not only ethical, it encourages authors to continue their creative work. This work is fully protected by copyright. No alterations, deletions or substitutions may be made in the work without the prior written consent of the publisher. No part of this work may be reproduced or transmitted in any form or by any means, electronic or mechanical, including photocopy, recording, videotape, film, or any information storage and retrieval system, without permission in writing from the publisher. It may not be performed either by professionals or amateurs without payment of royalty. All rights, including, but not limited to, the professional, motion picture, radio, television, videotape, foreign language, tabloid, recitation, lecturing, publication and reading, are reserved.

> For performance of any songs, music and recordings mentioned in this play which are in copyright, the permission of the copyright owners must be obtained or other songs and recordings in the public domain substituted.

©MMXI by
BONNIE ROBERTS
Based upon the book by
ELIZABETH VON ARNIM

Printed in the United States of America
All Rights Reserved
(THE ENCHANTED APRIL)

ISBN: 978-1-58342-706-4

For all the women who transformed my life:

Gail, Lesley, Rae, Pat, Melanie, Kristal, Annie,
my sister, Julia
and my mother, Ellen.

You are all my San Salvatore.

IMPORTANT BILLING AND CREDIT REQUIREMENTS

All producers of the play *must* give credit to the author of the play in all programs distributed in connection with performances of the play and in all instances in which the title of the play appears for purposes of advertising, publicizing or otherwise exploiting the play and/or a production. The name of the author *must* also appear on a separate line, on which no other name appears, immediately following the title, and *must* appear in size of type not less than fifty percent (50%) the size of the title type. Biographical information on the author, if included in the playbook, may be used in all programs. *In all programs this notice must appear:*

"Produced by special arrangement with
THE DRAMATIC PUBLISHING COMPANY of Woodstock, Illinois"

* * * *

The Enchanted April was first produced at Jackson County Comprehensive High School, Jefferson, Ga. The premiere performance was in April 2010 in the McMullan Auditorium at JCCHS. The cast was as follows:

Lotty Wilkins	Lindsey Slayton
Rose Arbuthnot	Ansley Moore
Mrs. Fisher	Amanda Seden
Lady Caroline Dester	Tori Dixon, Shelby Myers
Mellersh Wilkins	Steven Strickland
Frederick Arbuthnot	Robert Stephens
Mr. Briggs	Cody Ramey, Robert Sparrow
Beppo	Johnny Boddie
Francesca	Colleen Gearty

THE ENCHANTED APRIL

CHARACTERS:

LOTTY WILKINS . . . . early 30s
ROSE ARBUTHNOT. . . . . early 30s
MRS. FISHER . . . . late 50s, early 60s
LADY CAROLINE DESTER. . . . . early to mid-20s
MELLERSH WILKINS . . . . early 40s
FREDERICK ARBUTHNOT . . . . early 40s
MR. BRIGGS. . . . . mid- to late 30s
FRANCESCA. . . . . mid- to late 50s
BEPPO. . . . . early 30s

ADDITIONAL SERVANTS as needed.

NOTE: See back of script for expanded character descriptions.

SET AND TECHNICAL REQUIREMENTS:

ACT I

Areas for each location indicated by small groupings of furniture and pools of light set in front of the mid curtain. These areas include:

The Women's Club, the Arbuthnot's Parlor, the Wilkins' Dining Room, Mrs. Fisher's Sitting Room, Mr. Briggs' Sitting Room and Lady Caroline's Front Foyer. The Boat/Train/Carriage may be a simple bench and stool.

ACT II

Unit set. The garden terrace of San Salvatore. The JCCHS used a turntable for the dining area. The turret wall rotates to a dining area.

ACT I

(The sound of a heavy, steady rain is heard and continues throughout most of the act.

Lights up on the central area revealing a few armchairs, and perhaps an end table. ROSE ARBUTHNOT is sitting reading a newspaper. She does not look up as LOTTY WILKINS comes dashing in, frantically jotting notes in a small journal.)

LOTTY *writing).* To wounded soldier...sixpence. *(She looks around for a seat, takes off her coat shaking the drops of rain off, and looks across at ROSE who is reading the newspaper. She leans in and reads over ROSE's shoulder and gasps in surprise and pleasure. ROSE looks up at her and LOTTY realizes she is being rude. She sits, restlessly, and after a long moment, blurts out...)* Are you reading about the castle and the wisteria?
ROSE. I beg your pardon? Why do you ask me that?
LOTTY. Only because I saw it too, and I thought perhaps, somehow—the advertisement about the castle. It sounds so wonderful, doesn't it? *(She jumps up and points over ROSE's shoulder to the newspaper page. Reading aloud.)* To Those who appreciate Wisteria and Sunshine. Small mediaeval Italian Castle on the shores of the Med-

iterranean to be Let Furnished for the month of April. Necessary servants remain. Z, Box 1000, The Times. Can you just imagine it? It seems such a wonderful thing —this advertisement about the wisteria—and— It seems so wonderful—and it is such a miserable day...

ROSE. Perhaps it seems wonderful because of the miserable day...

LOTTY. I see you in church...every Sunday...

ROSE. In church?

LOTTY. I thought you looked like the paintings of a Madonna, only a sad one, you know, somewhat disappointed.

ROSE. A disappointed Madonna? Really, I...

LOTTY. You were reading it, weren't you?

ROSE. Yes...I...

LOTTY. Wouldn't it be wonderful?

ROSE. Wonderful, very wonderful, but it's no use wasting one's time thinking of such things.

LOTTY. Oh but it is! People think that such delights are only for the rich. Yet the advertisement is addressed to persons who appreciate castles and wisterias, you know, and so it is also addressed to me because I certainly appreciate them, more than anybody knows, more than I have ever told anybody...but...

ROSE. But?

LOTTY. Just considering the considering of them is worthwhile in itself—such a change from this dreary weather and Hampstead—and sometimes I believe I really do believe—if one considers hard enough, one gets things.

ROSE. Perhaps you will tell me your name. If we are to be friends, as I hope we are, we had better begin at the beginning. I am Rose Arbuthnot.

LOTTY. Oh, yes. How kind of you. I'm Mrs. Lotty Wilkins. I don't expect that it conveys anything to you. Sometimes it doesn't convey anything to me either. But I am Mrs. Wilkins. I never really liked that name. Wilkins. It's rather a small, mean name, with a kind of a facetious twist at the end like the upward curve of a pug dog's tail. There it is, however, there's no doing anything about it. My husband is a solicitor. He's…very handsome.

ROSE. That must be a great pleasure to you…

LOTTY. Why?

ROSE *(taken aback)*. Because…because beauty—handsomeness—is a gift like any other, and if it is properly used… *(She notices LOTTY staring intently outward.)* Lotty?

LOTTY *(leaning forward eagerly)*. Why don't we try and get it?

ROSE *(faintly)*. Get it?

LOTTY. Yes. Not just sit here and say "How wonderful" and then go home to Hampstead without having put out a finger—go home just as usual and see about dinner and fish just as we have been doing for years and years. In fact, I see no end to it. There is no end to it. So that there ought to be a break, there ought to be intervals—in everybody's interests. Why it would really be unselfish to go away and be happy for a little, because we would come back so much nicer. You see, after a bit, everybody needs a holiday.

ROSE. But how do you mean, get it?

LOTTY. Take it!

ROSE. Take it?

LOTTY. Rent it. Hire it. Have it!

ROSE. But…do you mean…you and I?

LOTTY. Yes! Between us. Share. Then it would only cost half, and you look so—you look exactly as if you wanted it as much as I do—as if you ought to have a rest—have something happy happen to you.

ROSE. Why…but we don't know each other.

LOTTY. But just think how well we would do if we went away together for a month! And I've saved for a rainy day, Mellersh insists I save, Mellersh is Mr. Wilkins, and I HAVE saved for a rainy day, and I expect so have you, and this IS a rainy day—look at it…

ROSE. But, Lotty… *(She thinks LOTTY may be a bit unbalanced.)*

LOTTY. Think of getting away for a whole month—from everything—to heaven—

ROSE. You shouldn't say things like that! The vicar…you see…heaven isn't somewhere else. It is here and now. We are told so. Heaven is in our home.

LOTTY. But it isn't!

ROSE *(desperately)*. It is there if we choose, if we make it.

LOTTY. I do choose, and I do not make it, and it isn't.

ROSE *(earnestly)*. I'd like so much to be friends. Won't you come and see me, or let me come see you sometimes? Whenever you feel as if you wanted to talk. I'll give you my address *(searches in her handbag)* and then you won't forget. *(She hands LOTTY a calling card.)*

LOTTY *(as if she hasn't heard her)*. It's so funny, but I see us both—you and me—this April in the medieval castle.

ROSE. Do you?

LOTTY. Don't you ever see things in a kind of flash before they happen?

ROSE. Never. *(She hesitates.)* Of course, it would be most beautiful, most beautiful.

LOTTY. Even if we are wrong, it would only be for a month.

ROSE. That...

LOTTY. Anyhow, I'm sure it's wrong to go on being good for too long, till one gets miserable. And I can see you've been good for years and years, because you look so unhappy. And I've done nothing but my duties, things for other people, ever since I was a little girl, and I don't believe that anyone loves me a bit—a bit the better—and I—oh I long for something else—something else. *(She frantically searches for a handkerchief in her handbag.)* Will you believe that I've never spoken to anyone before in my life like this? I can't think, I simply don't know what has come over me.

ROSE. It's the advertisement, I expect.

LOTTY. Yes, *(dabbing her eyes)* and us being so *(blowing nose)* miserable!

ROSE *(defensively, then calms herself)*. I am not miserable! *(Affected by LOTTY's sniffles.)* We must try to live our lives for the good of others if we... *(LOTTY sniffles again.)* We should place ourselves unreservedly in God's hands so that... *(LOTTY raises a tear-stained face to her.)* ...I suppose... *(weakening)* it would do no harm to answer the advertisement... *(LOTTY raises her head, smiling hopefully.)* Merely an inquiry, no commitment. *(LOTTY continues to smile warmly, a ray of sunshine.)* There's no harm in simply asking.

LOTTY. It isn't as if it committed us to anything. It only shows how immaculately good we have been all our lives. *(ROSE begins to write a note to the advertisement address.)* The very first time we do anything our husbands don't know about we feel guilty.

ROSE. I'm afraid I can't say I have been immaculately good.

LOTTY. Oh, but I am sure you have—I see you being good—and that's why you are not happy.

ROSE. You mustn't say things like that! I don't know why you insist that I am not happy. When you know me better I think you'll find that I am. And I am sure you don't really mean that goodness, if one could attain it, makes one unhappy.

LOTTY. Our sort of goodness does. We have attained it, and we are unhappy. There are miserable sorts of goodness and happy sorts—the sort we'll have at the medieval castle, for instance, is the happy sort.

ROSE. That is, supposing we go there. After all, we are just writing to ask. Anybody may do that. I think it quite likely we shall find conditions impossible, and even if they were not, probably by tomorrow, we shall not want to go.

LOTTY *(simply)*. I see us there.

(Blackout.

ROSE steps into a pool of light, her home, an armchair. She nervously sits, hands clasped tightly, as if in prayer.)

ROSE *(looking up)*. I feel I ought really to ask, straight out and roundly, that the medieval castle should already be taken by someone else. The whole thing settled. But I can't ask it. I can't risk it. After all, if I spend my present nest egg on a holiday I could quite soon accumulate another. All this is very unbalancing; it creates an unusually disturbed condition of mind. I feel happy. I feel guilty. And I feel afraid. Beauty. Beauty. Beauty. That word keeps ringing in my ears. I have never been to Italy. Still...to spend my nest egg on self-indulgence. To make myself happy? To suppose that I would ever forget my duties to the extent of drawing it out of the bank and spending it on myself. I am happy. I am! Surely I wouldn't, I couldn't ever do such a thing as that? Forget my poor, forget all the miserable and sick people in my parish as completely as that? Why is strength given to one if not to help us NOT do them? If I ask Frederick for the money, he will give it to me. The money he gets from writing those dreadful books. He'll be glad for me to go. He doesn't seem to bear the remotest resemblance to the original Frederick I knew. He doesn't seem to have the least need of any of the things he used to say were so important and beautiful...love...home...complete communion of thoughts...complete immersion in each of our interests. Then he began to write those books, those dreadful novels about fallen women. I tried so hard to remind him of the way we felt when we first married, the point at which we, hand in hand, so splendidly started. I don't dare think of him as he used to be in those marvelous first days of our marriage, before our child died... *(She wilts.)* The poor are my children. What could be happier than a life devoted to servitude? I am happy! I am! *(Softly.)* Perhaps...when we are both quite old...

(Lights fade on ROSE.

Up on LOTTY in her home.)

LOTTY. In the whole of my world I possess only ninety pounds. I saved it year to year, put it by pound by pound, out of my dress allowance. I scraped this sum together at the suggestion of my husband, Mr. Wilkins, as a shield and refuge against a rainy day. "You never know," Mr. Wilkins always says "when there will be a rainy day, and you may be very glad to find you have a nest egg. Indeed we both may." Mr. Wilkins, Mellersh, encourages thrift, except for his food. He even gave me a journal in which to write down every expense, sixpence for a wounded soldier, flowers for the table, although he thinks those a terrible waste of money. I wonder perhaps if this is the rainy day Mr. Wilkins, Mellersh, has so often encouraged me to prepare for? Perhaps this is what Providence had intended for me all along. Getting out of this horrid rain and going to a medieval castle in Italy, the Mediterranean in April and the wisteria... I've never been anywhere. *(She sighs.)* Mellersh and I go to parties of impressionist painters, of whom in Hampstead there are so many. I dread paintings. I never know what to say about them. I murmur "marvelous" and I hope that is enough. But then nobody minds me. Nobody listens. Nobody takes any notice of me...at parties or anywhere else for that matter. I am practically invisible, a reluctant conversationalist. I beg Mellersh to let me stay home. He pronounces absolutely intelligent judgments on arts and artists. He never says a word too much, nor a word too many. Mr. Wilkins, Mellersh, encourages me to say I am Mrs. Mellersh Wilkins. I only do that when he is within earshot. Once I told Mellersh that it only makes Wilkins sound worse, emphasizing it like the gate post of a villa only emphasizes the villa. *(This makes perfect sense to her.)* Mellersh replied, quite patiently, "I am not a villa." And he looked at me as if he thinks he may have married a fool. I told him, of course, he is not a villa. I never supposed he was. I had never dreamed of calling him a villa. It was a dreadful quarrel. He never raised his voice…just looked at me in dignified silence.

(Lights out LOTTY's area.

Lights up on LOTTY and ROSE in MR. BRIGGS' parlor.)

ROSE. Mr. Briggs is asking for references. I never dreamed we would require references.

LOTTY. Sixty pounds for a single month. One half of my nest egg.

ROSE. All I can see are boots.

LOTTY. Boots?

ROSE. All the stout boots I could buy for the orphans. And, Lotty, besides the rent there will be the servants' wages, the food, the railway journeys to and from and a boat to cross the channel…

LOTTY. But it is our very own money, and…

ROSE *(suddenly)*. Lotty, I have the entire sixty pounds in my bag. I shall tell the owner, Mr. Briggs, that I waive the right to only pay half. *(Notices LOTTY smiling.)* Lotty?

LOTTY. I think I have an idea as well.

ROSE. For what?

(She notices MR. BRIGGS coming in. She and LOTTY prepare to convince him.)

BRIGGS. Ladies! Do pardon me for keeping you waiting.

ROSE. We've come about San Salvatore. If it is still available I would like to pay in full waiving my right to put only a deposit down. I hope that will be satisfactory?

BRIGGS *(very affected by her charm, and fragile nature)*. Perhaps I could know the name of my new tenants?

ROSE. Oh! This is Mrs. Lotty Wilkins and I am Rose Arbuthnot. *(She hands BRIGGS the money hopefully.)*

BRIGGS. This is all very unusual. Please sit down. *(He goes to write a receipt.)* In this case, I will of course waive the need for any references for such charming ladies. Nasty day, isn't it? You'll find the old castle has plenty of sunshine, whatever else it hasn't got. Husband going?

ROSE *(startled)*. No.

BRIGGS. Oh I am so sorry. I didn't mean to intrude. The war I suppose? So sad. I am sorry.

ROSE. Yes.

BRIGGS *(handing her a receipt and smiling charmingly at her)*. Now, there you go. I am the richer and you're the happier. I've got the money and you have acquired San Salvatore for the month of April. I wonder who's got it best?

ROSE *(smiling gently back)*. I think you know.

BRIGGS. I hope you'll like the old place. *(Hands ROSE a set of old keys.)* In April, you know, it's simply a mass of flowers. And then there's the sea. You must wear white. *(LOTTY gasps in excitement. He turns to her as if noticing her for the first time.)* You both must, of

Act I   THE ENCHANTED APRIL   17

course. You'll fit in very well. *(Turning back to ROSE.)* There are several portraits of you there.

ROSE. Portraits?

BRIGGS. Madonnas, you know. There's one on the stairs really exactly like you.

ROSE. Are they looking disappointed?

BRIGGS. Why, no.

LOTTY *(a gush of emotion)*. Oh! Thank you Mr. Briggs!

ROSE *(also rising)*. Yes, thank you, Mr. Briggs.

BRIGGS. Here are the keys. San Salvatore awaits. *(They shake hands graciously and leave. He watches them go.)* Such a beautiful woman. Yet sad. Perhaps I should have asked for those references…she probably thought me the perfect fool, not a businessman at all.

(Lights out on Briggs parlor.

Up on LOTTY and ROSE outside MR. BRIGGS townhome.)

LOTTY. Rose!
ROSE *(startled)*. What?
LOTTY. We've done it!

(They clasp hands and jump like schoolgirls.)

ROSE *(suddenly still)*. Our nest eggs almost all gone.

LOTTY. I saw a way out of that difficulty. Now that we have acquired San Salvatore, the beautiful…sounds almost religious, doesn't it?… San Salvatore, it fascinates me…we can in turn, advertise in the Agony Column of *The Times*, to inquire after two more ladies, with similar desires to our own, to join us and share the expenses. *(ROSE hesitates.)* We could economize on the food... gather olives off the olive trees...they're our olives, for a while at least...and perhaps catch fish.

ROSE. Two more ladies? *(Thinks for a moment.)* That's a splendid idea, Lotty. We could perhaps advertise for more ladies to join us but perhaps having so many would not be so peaceful.

(Lights out on ROSE and LOTTY, then fade up on Women's Club area as they walk in.)

ROSE. There seems to be only two ladies in England at this moment who have any wish to join us. We have had only TWO answers to our advertisement!

LOTTY. Well, we only want two. Although I had imagined a great rush...

ROSE. I think choice would have been a good thing.

LOTTY. You mean because then we needn't have had Lady Caroline Dester.

ROSE. I didn't say that.

LOTTY. We needn't have her. Just one more person would help us a great deal with the rent. We're not obliged to have two.

ROSE. But why should we not have her? She seems really quite what we want.

LOTTY. Yes. She does from her letter. I feel I will be terribly shy. I have never come across any members of the aristocracy, not in Hampstead at least. *(Notices Lady CAROLINE entering.)* Oh! Here she comes.

ROSE *(rising to shake CAROLINE's hand)*. How pleasant to meet you, Lady Caroline. I am Rose Arbuthnot and this is Mrs. Wilkins. Please do sit down.

CAROLINE. Thank you. *(Removes coat, to reveal chic fashionable dress.)*

ROSE *(after glancing at LOTTY who is starstruck)*. Lady Caroline, you understand that it will only be the four of us at San Salvatore. It will be very quiet and peaceful there.

CAROLINE *(so charming and pleasant that ROSE and LOTTY cannot take offence)*. That is exactly what I am longing for. I desire to get away from everybody I have ever known. I will be in Italy, a place I absolutely adore. I will not be in a hotel...I loathe places like that, don't you? *(ROSE nods slowly. LOTTY nods quickly.)* I will not be staying with friends, people I dislike. I will be in the company of strangers who will not be mentioning a single person I could possibly know. It all seems most restful.

ROSE. I suppose everything is in order, then? Lotty?

(LOTTY just smiles faintly and nods.)

CAROLINE *(rising)*. I will see you in San Salvatore then.

(Holds out her hand to ROSE, then LOTTY. ROSE shakes it. LOTTY starts to curtsy. ROSE stops her. CAROLINE looks startled, smiles, then moves to the side to put her coat on.)

LOTTY. She's beautiful.
ROSE. Yes, she is. *(They both sigh and exit.)*

CAROLINE. It seems a restful thing to know that I am going to spend an entire month with women who wear dresses made, I dimly recall, over five summers ago. I am having a violent reaction against beautiful clothes and the slavery they impose on one. My experience is that the instant one has got beautiful clothes they take one in hand and give one no peace till they have been everywhere and been seen by everybody. I need a rest. For a long time now I have felt that my life is nothing but a noise, so much so that I feel must get out of earshot for a little while or I will be completely and perhaps permanently deafened. But suppose it was only a noise about nothing? I have not had a question like that in my mind before. It makes me feel lonely. I want to be alone, not lonely. That is very different, that is something that aches and hurts dreadfully. It is what I dread most. It makes me go to so many parties, to block out the noise. Lately even the parties have not seemed to protect me at all. It is possible that loneliness has nothing to do with the circumstances but in how one meets them? It's very curious, but I just want time to think. I have never wanted to do that before. Sometimes I feel as if I don't even belong to myself, not my own at all, just some universal thing, a sort of beauty-of-all-work. What does one do with men once one has got them? None of them talk to me of anything but love. How foolish and fatiguing that becomes after a bit. When they propose to me, I ask them "WHY should I love you? Why should I?" I never get an answer. I feel like a wasp caught in honey and I can't seem to unstick my wings no matter how desperately I try. The War finished me. It killed the one man I have ever felt safe with, whom I would have married. He's dead. And I have never felt so lonely in my life.

(She turns and steps into the area for her home. FREDERICK ARBUTHNOT, pseudonym Frederick Arundel, is sitting on a chair holding one of his books. He nervously whistles or hums looking around, waiting. Lady CAROLINE walks in.)

FREDERICK *(rising)*. Caroline! You look lovely! *(He attempts to kiss her hand. She turns it into a handshake.)*

CAROLINE *(aloof)*. Frederick Arundel. What brings you to my mother's home, again? Ah, I see you have brought Mother another one of your books. How lovely of you.

FREDERICK. How are you, Caroline? Actually, the book is for you. *(Attempts to hand it to her. She avoids it, getting her hat, gloves and coat off.)* Your mother has invited a few of her friends over for dinner. Will you be joining us?

CAROLINE *(hesitating)*. I think not, Frederick.

FREDERICK *(hopeful)*. Would you prefer dining out?

CAROLINE. I prefer to be alone this evening. In fact, I will be taking a holiday very soon. Alone. Thank you for your lovely invitation, however. Good evening, Frederick. *(She smiles fondly and exits.)*

FREDERICK *(watches her go. Then straightens tie and mutters to himself as if practicing)*. Ah, Lady Dester, I understand your daughter is taking a holiday soon. Will you be going with her?

(Lights out on FREDERICK.

Lights fade up on ROSE and LOTTY in MRS. FISHER's sitting room.)

LOTTY. But if she can't come to the club, how can she go to Italy?
ROSE. We shall hear that from her own lips.

(They look around but do not see MRS. FISHER enter.)

MRS. FISHER. I knew them all, you know.
ROSE. Good afternoon, Mrs. Fisher. This is Mrs. Wilkins and I am Mrs. Arbuthnot.
MRS. FISHER. I am the perfect companion for your trip, Mrs. Arbuthnot. I am a widow of eleven years. I only ask to be allowed to sit quietly in the sun and remember better times.
LOTTY *(pointing to the pictures)*. Are they famous?
MRS. FISHER. These are all signed photographs of illustrious Victorian dead, all of whom I have known since I was little. In my father's house, an eminent critic before his death, practically everybody who was anybody in letters and arts came into our household. *(Swinging her cane toward a picture.)* Carlyle scowled at me. *(Swings cane in another direction, pointing.)* Matthew Arnold held me on his knee while reciting. *(Cane points to another frame.)* Tennyson teased me about the length of my pigtail.
ROSE *(trying to return to the point)*. There are lovely gardens at San Salvatore, Mrs. Fisher, and …
MRS. FISHER. I am very fond of flowers, too. I remember once when I was spending a weekend with my father at Box Hill…

LOTTY *(excited about meeting someone who knew famous people)*. Who lives at Box Hill?

MRS. FISHER *(rather shortly)*. Meredith, of course. I remember a particular weekend, my father often took me, but I remember this weekend particularly...

LOTTY *(interrupting eagerly)*. Did you know Keats? *(ROSE attempts to quell LOTTY's exuberance.)*

MRS. FISHER *(after a pause, with sub-acid reserve)*. No. I was not acquainted with Keats or with William Shakespeare.

LOTTY *(nervously, knows she has made a mistake)*. Oh, of course! How ridiculous of me! It's because... *(ROSE again attempts to quell LOTTY.)* It's because the immortals seem somehow to be alive, don't they? As if they were here, going to walk into the room in another minute and one forgets they are dead. In fact, one knows perfectly well they are not dead, not nearly so dead as even you and I now. *(MRS. FISHER stares over her glasses at LOTTY.)* I thought I saw Keats the other day. In Hampstead—crossing the road in front of that house—you know—the house where he lived—

ROSE. We really must be going, Mrs. Fisher...

LOTTY. I really thought I saw him...he was dressed in a...

ROSE *(gently)*. Lotty, we will be late for lunch.

MRS. FISHER. I believe now is a good time to ask for references. *(ROSE and LOTTY are startled.)* It is usual.

LOTTY. But oughtn't we be asking for references from you?

MRS. FISHER *(handing an embossed card to ROSE)*. These ought to be sufficient.

ROSE. The president of the Royal Academy, the archbishop of Canterbury, the governor of the Bank of England...

MRS. FISHER. They have known me since I was little.

LOTTY *(bursts out courageously)*. I don't think references are nice things at all between—between ordinary decent people. We are not business people. We needn't distrust each other.

ROSE *(handing back the card, sweetly)*. I am afraid references do bring a certain atmosphere into our holiday plan that isn't quite what we want, and I don't think we'll take yours up or give you any ourselves. So that I suppose you won't wish to join us. *(Holds out her hand in good-bye.)*

MRS. FISHER *(grudgingly)*. Very well. I waive references. For you. Are there any other women selected for our traveling companions?

LOTTY. Lady Caroline Dester is...

MRS. FISHER. Is she a widow, too?

LOTTY. Oh no! She can't be a widow. She hasn't married yet!

ROSE. Lady Caroline is somewhat younger but assures us that she is simply seeking quiet and solitude, much like yourself. Lotty, we must go. We will be late for lunch.

MRS. FISHER. Forgive me if I do not see you out. My stick prevents me from getting about easily.

ROSE. Good afternoon, Mrs. Fisher. *(She quickly turns and guides LOTTY out before she can say anything.)*

MRS. FISHER *(after watching LOTTY and ROSE leave)*. I am well off and have the desire for comforts proper to my age, but I dislike expenses. If I had so chosen, I could have lived in an opulent part of London and

Act I   THE ENCHANTED APRIL   25

driven from it and to it in a Rolls-Royce. I have no such wish. Worries attend such possessions, worries of every kind, crowned by bills. In the sobriety of Prince of Wales Terrace I can enjoy inexpensive yet real comfort, without being snatched at by predatory men-servants or collectors for charities, and a taxi stand is at the end of the road. My annual outlay is small. This house was inherited. Death had furnished it for her. I walk in the dining room on the Turkey carpet of my father; I regulated my day by the excellent black marble clock on the mantelpiece which I remember from childhood; my walls were entirely covered by the photographs my illustrious deceased friends had given either me or my father, with their own handwriting across the lower parts of their bodies, and the windows shrouded by the maroon curtains of all my life, are decorated besides with the selfsame aquariums to which I owe my first lessons in sea lore, and in which still swam slowly the goldfishes of my youth. *(Stares toward the goldfish bowl.)* Are they the same goldfish? I do not know. Perhaps, like carp, they outlive everybody. Perhaps, on the other hand, behind the deep-sea vegetation provided for them at the bottom, they have from time to time as the years have gone by withdrawn and replaced themselves. Sometimes when I sit at my solitary meals I wonder if they might not be the same goldfish that had that day been there when Carlyle—how well I remember it—angrily strode up to them in the middle of some argument with my father that had grown heated, and striking the glass smartly with his fist had put them to flight, shouting as they fled, "Och, ye deaf deevils! Och, ye lucky deaf deevils! Ye can't hear anything of the blasted, blethering, doddering, glaikit fool-stuff yer maister talks, can ye?" Or words to that effect. *(She collects herself, realizing that she may have become too emotional.)* Dear, great-souled Carlyle. Such true freshness; such real grandeur. Rugged, if you will—yes, undoubtedly sometimes rugged, and startling in a drawing room, but magnificent. Who is there now to put beside him? Who is there to mention in the same breath? And here is this generation; this generation of puniness, raising its little voice in doubts, or, still worse, not giving itself the trouble to raise it at all, not—it is incredible, even reading him. I do not read him either, but that is different. I have read his work. Of course I have read him. Yes, I must have read him. *(Pause.)* Though sometimes the details escape me.

(Lights out on MRS. FISHER's sitting room.

Lights fade up on the Arbuthnot and Wilkins homes revealing FREDERICK sitting in an armchair reading and MELLERSH sitting at his dining room table. LOTTY brings dessert in on a tray and fusses over placing things in front of MELLERSH. He is delighted by this wifely attention.)

MELLERSH *(condescendingly)*. Dinner was perfect, my dear. Quite perfect. Lotty, I have been thinking of taking you on a holiday to Italy in April. Having noticed the peculiar persistent vileness of the weather, I have conceived of the notion to get away from England for the Easter. I am doing very well in my business. We can afford the trip. Switzerland is useless in April but there is something familiar-sounding about Easter in Italy. So to Italy we will go. Besides, taking you with will be quite useful, a second person is always useful in a country whose language one does not speak. *(LOTTY squeaks and jumps back with the tray then stands staring in shock.)* Did you not hear me, Lotty? I am thinking of taking you to Italy for Easter.

LOTTY. That is quite extraordinary, Mellersh, an extraordinary coincidence, really most extraordinary. I was just going to tell you that I have been invited, a friend has invited me...Easter...Easter was in April, too, wasn't it? My friend has a house there.

MELLERSH. I don't believe you! What friend? You don't have any friends, Lotty!

LOTTY. I do now. Mrs. Rose Arbuthnot. She is my friend and she has invited me to Italy for April.

MELLERSH *(indignant)*. I don't know any Rose Arbuthnot! Who is she?

LOTTY. She's a very nice woman, a Madonna...

MELLERSH. A WHAT!?

LOTTY. There are paintings of her at this house.

MELLERSH. The Madonna?

LOTTY. No, Rose...well, yes, the Madonna, who looks like Rose, I mean Rose looks like her, only disappointed.

MELLERSH. You are NOT going to Italy with this Mrs. Arbuthnot, of whom I have never heard. I demand that you refuse the invitation.

LOTTY. It's all settled, Mellersh.

MELLERSH. It is nothing of the kind! Since you so outrageously accepted this invitation without consulting me, you will write and cancel your acceptance at once.

LOTTY. I will not write to cancel my acceptance!

MELLERSH. I am telling you, as your husband, you will cancel your acceptance of this invitation!

LOTTY. I want to go! And I AM going! *(She storms off.)*

MELLERSH *(throwing down his napkin and storming after her)*. LOTTY!

(Lights out on the Wilkins home.

Lights up on the Arbuthnot home.

ROSE enters timidly and stands behind FREDERICK's chair for a moment.)

ROSE. Frederick?

FREDERICK. Rose, my dear!

ROSE. I am thinking of taking a holiday with friends and...

FREDERICK. Delightful my dear! A holiday is just what you need! When do you leave?

ROSE. April. *(Hesitates.)* Frederick, I would be grateful if you would let me have some funds, some money for the trip, I...

FREDERICK *(rising, taking out wallet)*. Of course, my dear! You have only to ask. I will be working on my new book and you know how busy my schedule gets when I am working. I am only too pleased for you to go. I would not mind it in the very least. *(He leans forward to kiss her on the cheek, she flinches away.)*

ROSE. I thought you wouldn't mind. Thank you. *(She turns away, hurt that he is so glad to see her go.)*

FREDERICK *(turning back to newspaper to hide his hurt that she still is so distant to him)*. Have a splendid time, my dear. Don't hurry home while you are enjoying yourself.

ROSE. I'll stay if you need me, Frederick.

FREDERICK. Don't be silly, Rose! What a splendid opportunity for you! A holiday with friends.

ROSE. Yes, a holiday. I am going for a month's holiday. I need the rest. Gladys, our parlormaid, will see that you have meals and... *(She trails off. He is not listening.)* Good night, Frederick. *(She leaves.)*

FREDERICK *(after a moment)*. Hhmmm? Oh, good night, Rose.

(Lights out in Arbuthnot home.

Lights up center.

A solitary bench sits center. It will become various modes of transportation/scenery/locales.

A boat whistle is heard. Seagulls flying.

LOTTY and ROSE enter struggling with suitcases and hat boxes.)

LOTTY. We've been too good. Much too good, and that's why we feel as if we are doing wrong. We're browbeaten—we're not any longer real human beings. Real human beings aren't ever as good as we have been. Oh, to think how we ought to be happy now, here at the very station, actually starting, and we're not, and it's being spoilt for us just because we have spoilt them! What have we done—what have we done I should like to know, except for once want to go away by ourselves and have a rest from them!

ROSE. Lotty, please sit down. The boat is pulling away.

(LOTTY sits. They hold their hats as if in high wind, look at each other, and turn to retch over the "railing" behind them.

Lights out.

The sound of a train chugging down the tracks. A train whistle.

Lights up to reveal ROSE and LOTTY struggling again with suitcases and hat boxes as if walking the aisle of a rollicking train.)

ROSE *(trying to cheer LOTTY up)*. At least we can be happy that we are not seasick anymore. We've had a lovely lunch of filets of sole. We managed to catch our train for Turin, even though the train from Paris was late.

LOTTY. I have eaten a fish Mellersh wasn't eating. None of the porters in Paris or Turin knew Mellersh, and by tomorrow this lovely train will have taken us to Italy where we can leave all that dreariness behind!

(Thunder booms.

Both ladies look at each other, startled, then look up, dismayed, as they hear rain begin to fall on the roof of the train.

Lights out.

More thunder and heavy rain.

Lights up to reveal ROSE and LOTTY standing near the bench trying to shelter themselves from the rain.

Train sounds fade in the distance.)

ROSE. It's raining. How is this different?
LOTTY. This is Italian rain. *(Another clap of thunder.)* With Italian thunder. *(A pause to look around.)* Mr. Briggs said "You get out at Mezzago, and then you drive." There is no one here to drive.
ROSE. We are four hours late.

(Suddenly a man [BEPPO] darts out and sets a small bench slightly to the side and front of the ladies' bench. [This will be his driver's seat.] He grabs their suitcases reinstalling them in the "carriage" [behind the bench]. The ladies shriek and try to stop him, perhaps hitting him with their purses. His Italian is quite fast but presently they hear him shouting "San Salvatore.")

ROSE *(reaching out to stop LOTTY)*. Lotty, NO! He said "San Salvatore"!
BEPPO. Si, San Salvatore!

(Another thunderclap.

The ladies shriek and climb into the carriage.

BEPPO clicks the whip at an unseen horse. The horse whinnies. The carriage dashes off and they bump and sway side to side.

Rain and thunder continue.)

ROSE *(shouting to be heard)*. We don't know if he is taking us there.

LOTTY *(shouting)*. No. We don't know.

ROSE. I feel very uncomfortable.

LOTTY. It's so late.

ROSE. It's so dark.

LOTTY. The road is so lonely.

ROSE. Suppose a wheel comes off!

LOTTY. Suppose we meet Fascisti! *(ROSE looks at her, startled.)* Or the opposite of Fascisti!

ROSE. I am sorry we did not stop in Genoa and come on the next morning in daylight.

LOTTY. But that would have been the first of April.

ROSE. It is that now.

BEPPO. *Non preoccupi le signore. Il mio cavallo è un buon cavallo. Lo porterà sicuro a San Salvatore.* (Don't worry, ladies. My horse is a good horse. She will bring you safely to San Salvatore.)

LOTTY. I wish my mother had made me learn Italian when I was little.

ROSE. Then you could say "Please sit round the right way and look after the horse."

LOTTY. I don't even know what horse is in Italian!

ROSE. It is contemptible to be so ignorant.

(BEPPO turns around again, speaking Italian vociferously.)

BEPPO. *State bene? Potrei andare più velocemente se desiderate.* (Are you comfortable? I could go faster if you wish.)

LOTTY & ROSE. NO! NO! Turn around! Watch the horse! Not so FAST!

BEPPO. *Presto? Si! Si! Molto presto!* (Faster? Yes! Yes! We can go faster!) *(He whips the horse a bit to go faster! The ladies shriek and fall back. More thunder and lightning.)*

ROSE *(shouting to be heard)*. We shall be there in a minute!

LOTTY *(shouting also)*. We shall soon stop now.

(Suddenly the carriage stops. The rain is lessening. Several SERVANTS come out to get their bags, snatching and running off. ROSE and LOTTY try to get their attention by saying "San Salvatore." The SERVANTS repeat "Si, si, San Salvatore.")

LOTTY. This can't be San Salvatore.

ROSE. I don't think it can be. We can do nothing if these wicked people are determined to have our suitcases. We are both in God's hands.

LOTTY. I am afraid. *(They get out of the carriage.)* If only we had learned Italian when we were little.

ROSE. Then we could have said "We wish to be driven to the door."

LOTTY. But we don't even know the Italian for "door."

ROSE. Such ignorance is not only contemptible, *(looks around)* but definitely dangerous!

(BEPPO returns with an open umbrella that he holds over their heads.)

LOTTY. Perhaps it is all right. Surely, if he were going to rob us he would not be so courteous as to hold an umbrella over our heads to protect us from the rain.

BEPPO. San Salvatore! San Salvatore!

ROSE. There? *(Pointing up and to the wings, as if up a long hill.)*

BEPPO. *Si, si,* San Salvatore!

(LOTTY and ROSE come closer to BEPPO and peer up in the direction he is now pointing. They have hopeful looks on their faces as the rain and the lights dim.)

END OF ACT I

ACT II

(As the curtain opens, we see the terrace of San Salvatore. The morning sun is shining brightly, flowers are everywhere. A large oleander tree is in the back corner. The sounds of birds and soft ocean waves mingle. After a moment, LOTTY runs out on stage in her simple white muslin nightgown. She rushes to center stage and slowly spins around taking in the absolute beauty.)

LOTTY *(a long release of breath)*. Oh! *(She runs to the tree and then to flowers and then like a butterfly to any of the other delights on the terrace.)* So beautiful! And I am here to see it! So beautiful! And I am ALIVE to feel it! How beautiful. Not to have died before this...to have been allowed to see...breathe...feel this! It's as though I can hardly stay inside my self! Oh! Happy! No...poor ordinary, everyday word. It's as though I have been washed through with light. How astonishing to feel this sheer bliss. I am here, not doing, and not going to do a single unselfish thing, not going to do a single thing I don't want to do! I should feel a twinge... *(She pauses, then giggles.)* No, not one twinge! I have taken off all my goodness and left it behind me like a heap of rain-sodden clothes! Oh! *(A sudden thought.)* Mellersh. *(She closes her eyes and tries to think of him.)* I can't see him... How extraordinary not to be able to visualize Mellersh in Hampstead... I can't see him as he was...I can only see him here...all rose colored, resolved into violet, blue, almost iridescent. Mellersh...here?

ROSE *(to herself)*. Oh, good heavens, what does she see now?

LOTTY *(turns to ROSE, beatific smile and sincere)*. We are in God's hands!

ROSE *(worried, rushing to her)*. Oh! Why? What has happened? *(LOTTY simply smiles.)* I hope nothing has happened!

LOTTY *(smiling at her)*. How funny!

ROSE. What is funny?

LOTTY. We are. This is. Everything. It's all so wonderful. It's so funny and so adorable that we should be in it! I daresay when we finally reach heaven—the one they talk about so much—we shan't find it a bit more beautiful!

ROSE *(relaxing)*. Isn't it divine?

LOTTY. Were you ever, ever in your life so happy?

ROSE *(surprised)*. No! I am happy at this moment...the kind of happiness that just accepts, just breathes, just is...for the moment.

LOTTY. Let's go and look at that tree close. I don't believe it can only be a tree.

(LOTTY and ROSE start to head for the tree, look down, see that they are in their nightgowns and exit back into the house, laughing.

CAROLINE appears at the other side of the garden. BEPPO brings out a lawn chair and makes a fuss over opening it and placing it for CAROLINE's comfort.)

CAROLINE. Beppo?
BEPPO. *Si, signora? Lascilo spostare la sedia dal sole!* (Yes, miss? Would you like me to move the chair from the sun?)
CAROLINE. *Non, non, Beppo, mi excusa... La sedia e benissimo.* (No, Beppo, excuse me. The chair is fine.)
BEPPO. *Voi gradicono un parasole?* (Would you like a parasol?)
CAROLINE. *Non, ho bisogno di un parasole.* (No, I don't need a parasol.)
BEPPO. *Si, signora! Bellissimo! Bene...bene...* (Yes, miss. Beautiful. Good...good...) *(Finally he sets the chair down and leaves, bowing to CAROLINE as he exits.)*

(CAROLINE sinks into it and sits back, closing her eyes.

ROSE and LOTTY reenter, wearing soft, flowing, white dresses. They notice CAROLINE in her chaise.)

ROSE. She's going to get a headache sitting there in the sun like that.
LOTTY. She ought to have a hat.
ROSE. She's got her feet in the lilies.
LOTTY. They are hers as much as ours.
ROSE. Only one-fourth of them. *(They cross to CAROLINE. She looks up at them.)* Good morning!
CAROLINE. Good morning.
ROSE. We didn't know you had arrived.

CAROLINE. I got here yesterday morning.

ROSE. It's a great pity, because we were going to choose the nicest room for you.

CAROLINE. Oh, but I've done that. At least I think it's the nicest. It looks two ways—I adore a room that looks two ways, don't you?

LOTTY. And we meant to make it pretty for you with flowers.

CAROLINE. Francesca and Beppo have already done that. I told them directly I got here. Francesca is our housekeeper and Beppo does the gardening. They're wonderful.

ROSE. It's a good thing, of course, to be independent, and to know exactly what one wants.

CAROLINE. Yes. It saves trouble.

LOTTY. But one shouldn't be so independent as to leave no opportunity for other people to be nice to one. *(A pause.)* I didn't realize you were so pretty.

CAROLINE *(startled)*. It's very kind of you to think so.

LOTTY. Why, you're lovely, quite, quite lovely.

ROSE. I hope you make the most of it.

CAROLINE *(startled again)*. Oh, yes, I make the most of it. I've been doing that as long as I can remember.

ROSE. Because it won't last.

CAROLINE. I know. *(A gong is heard from inside the house.)* That would be Mrs. Fisher calling you to breakfast. I've already had mine.

(CAROLINE sits back in the chaise, closing her eyes. A dismissal. ROSE and LOTTY look at each other, then are startled by the gong clanging again. They dash toward the villa.

Act II   THE ENCHANTED APRIL   39

The dining room is revealed. MRS. FISHER is ensconced at the head of the table, a small gong at her side. FRANCESCA [the housemaid] is serving breakfast. ROSE and LOTTY cross to the table.)

ROSE. Oh.

LOTTY. Why, but it's like having the bread snatched out of one's mouth!

MRS. FISHER *(startled)*. How do you do. I can't get up because of my stick.

ROSE. We had no idea you were here.

MRS. FISHER. Yes. I am here.

LOTTY. It's a great disappointment. We had meant to give you such a welcome.

MRS. FISHER. I arrived yesterday with Lady Caroline.

LOTTY. It's really dreadful. There's nobody left to get anything ready for now. I feel thwarted. I feel as if the bread has been taken out of my mouth just when I was going to be happy swallowing it.

MRS. FISHER *(banging small mallet on gong. FRANCESCA appears)*. Francesca, *portimi un po'più di latte, per favore.* (Bring me some more milk, please.)

LOTTY. I was just thinking of cuckoos. *(A pause. ROSE and MRS. FISHER don't know what to say.)* Have you smelled the freesias? Freesias in London are quite beyond my budget. Occasionally I go into a shop and ask what they cost just so I can have an excuse to lift up a bunch and smell them, knowing all the time the cost was something awful like a shilling for about three flowers. Here they are just everywhere, bursting out of every corner. Imagine it, having freesias to pick in armfuls if you want to, with glorious sunshine flooding everywhere, in comfortable summer frocks and it being on the first of April! I suppose you realize, don't you, that we've gone to heaven?

MRS. FISHER. You're very young, aren't you?

ROSE. I hope your room is very comfortable.

MRS. FISHER. Quite. Will you have more coffee?

ROSE *(a bit competitive over hostess duties)*. No, thank you. Will you?

MRS. FISHER. No, thank you. There were two beds in my bedroom, filling it up unnecessarily. I had one taken out. It has made it much more convenient.

LOTTY. Oh! That's why I've got two beds in my room.

ROSE. I have two in my room as well.

MRS. FISHER. Your second one must be Lady Caroline's. She had hers removed as well. It seemed foolish to have more beds in a room than there are occupiers.

LOTTY. But we haven't got any husbands here either and I don't see any use in extra beds in one's room if one hasn't got husbands to put in them.

MRS. FISHER. Beds cannot be removed from one room after another. They must remain somewhere. In my day, husbands were taken seriously, as the only real obstacles to sin. Beds were not discussed and a decent reserve prevented them and husbands ever being spoken of in the same breath. *(Turning to ROSE.)* Do let me give you a little more coffee.

ROSE. No, thank you. But won't you have some more?

MRS. FISHER. No, indeed. I never have more than two cups at breakfast. Would you like an orange?

ROSE. No thank you. Would you?

Act II   THE ENCHANTED APRIL   41

MRS. FISHER. No I don't eat fruit at breakfast. It is an American fashion which I am too old now to adopt. Have you had all you want?

ROSE. Quite. Have you?

MRS. FISHER. Is this a habit of yours, this answering a question with a question? *(ROSE starts to retort.)* No, perhaps not.

LOTTY *(trying to intervene)*. I'm going to have one of these marvelous oranges. Rose, how can you resist them? Look—have this one...

ROSE. No, I'm going to see to my duties. *(Rising.)* You'll forgive me for leaving, won't you? What time would you like to have lunch?

MRS. FISHER. Lunch is at half past twelve.

ROSE. You shall have it at half past twelve then. I'll tell the cook. It will be a great struggle, but I've brought a little Italian dictionary.

MRS. FISHER. The cook knows.

ROSE. Oh?

MRS. FISHER. Lady Caroline has already told her. Lady Caroline speaks the kind of Italian cooks understand. I am prevented going to the kitchen because of my stick. And even if I were able to go, I fear I shouldn't be understood.

ROSE. But—

LOTTY. But it's too wonderful! Why we've got positively nothing to do here, either of us, except be happy. You wouldn't believe how terribly good Rose and I have been for years without stopping, and how much we need a perfect rest. *(She drags ROSE out of the dining room.)*

MRS. FISHER. Well, I never!

(Lights out in the dining room area.

Lights up in the garden on the terrace.)

LOTTY. Don't you see that if someone else does the ordering it frees us?

ROSE. Yes. I do see that. However, I think it rather silly to have everything taken out of our hands.

LOTTY. I love things to be taken out of my hands.

ROSE. But we found San Salvatore and it is rather silly that Mrs. Fisher should behave as if it only belonged to her.

LOTTY. What is rather silly is to mind. I can't see the least point in being in authority at the price of one's liberty.

ROSE. Yes. *(Sighs.)*

LOTTY. You mustn't sigh in heaven. One doesn't.

ROSE. I was thinking how one longs to share this with those one loves.

LOTTY. You mustn't long in heaven. You're supposed to be complete there. And it is, heaven, isn't it, Rose? See how all the different flowers are let in together, the dandelions and the irises, the vulgar and the superior, me and Mrs. Fisher, all of us welcome, all mixed together and all happy!

ROSE. Mrs. Fisher doesn't seem happy, not visibly, anyhow.

LOTTY. She'll begin soon, you'll see.

ROSE. I don't believe that after a certain age one begins anything.

LOTTY. No one, however old or tough, can resist the effects of perfect beauty. Mrs. Fisher will leave off being

Act II THE ENCHANTED APRIL 43

ossified, go all soft and I shouldn't be surprised if we get quite fond of her. *(Laughing in joy.)*

ROSE. Perhaps. *(Notices Lady CAROLINE still in her chair. Waving.)* Hello!

(CAROLINE waves slightly, closes her eyes and lays back in her chair.)

LOTTY. If we weren't in heaven, I would say we had been snubbed.

ROSE. Perhaps she is unhappy.

LOTTY. Whatever it is, she will get over it here.

ROSE. We must try and help her.

LOTTY. Oh, no! Nobody helps anybody in heaven. That's finished with. You don't try to be or do. You simply are. *(She takes ROSE by the hand and walks out through an arbor.)*

(FRANCESCA enters from the doors and looks for Lady CAROLINE. When she spies her in the garden, she dashes over to her. She is trying to find someone to tell her what to cook for lunch and dinner.)

FRANCESCA. *Mi excusa! Vorrei conoscere che cosa cucinare per pranzo. Ho chiesto alla vostra madre ma mi non ha ditto.* (I would like to know what to cook for lunch. I asked your mother but she did not tell me.)

CAROLINE. She is NOT my mother... *Excusa. Non e la mia madre!*

FRANCESCA. *Sono felice lei non sono la vostra madre.* (I am very glad she is not your mother!)

CAROLINE. *Ripari qualunque gradite. Sono sicuro che sarà fine. Voglio appena essere lasciato solo.* (Fix whatever you like. I prefer to be left alone.)

FRANCESCA. *Meraviglioso! Preparerò una festività!* (Marvelous! I will prepare a feast!) *(She exits quickly.)*

CAROLINE. Go away! *(Notices she is gone.)* Just like the fly in my bedroom this morning. It was determined to settle on my face and no matter how many times I tried to swat it, the pest eluded me and I ended up hitting myself in the face! It kept coming back, buzzing and then skimming gracefully away. I should have told Francesca to put a net around my bed. People are exactly like flies. I wish I had a net to keep them off. At first it seemed that San Salvatore would be the one place I could be left alone! First Beppo, constantly asking where I would like my chair, would I like a parasol, do I require fresh water or lemonade? Then Francesca asking about the dining arrangements! Will I never get away from being waited on, from being made comfortable, being asked where I want things put, having to say "Thank you."

BEPPO *(entering quickly)*. *Scusilo. Il sole sta importunandolo?* (Excuse me! Is the sun bothering you?) *(He picks up her parasol and holds it over her head. Smiles.)*

CAROLINE. *Non! (Gets up and holds out her hand for the parasol.) Penso che vada per una camminata. Scusilo.* (No! I think I will go for a walk. Excuse me.)

BEPPO. *Si, signorina. (They exit.)*

MRS. FISHER *(entering)*. What I want, what I surely have a right to, is privacy! I have no wish to intrude on the others; why then should they intrude on me? I could always relax my privacy if, when I become more acquainted with my companions, I think it would be worthwhile. *(Pause.)* I doubt whether any of the three will develop enough to make me think it worthwhile. *(Pause.)* Hardly anything is really worthwhile, except the past. It is astonishing, simply amazing, the superiority of the past to the present. My friends in London, solid persons of my own age, know the same past I know, can talk about it with me, could compare it, as I do, to the present. In remembering those great men, we can forget for a moment these trivial and barren young people who still, in spite of the war, seem to litter the world in such numbers. I haven't come away from these friends to chat away with three persons of another generation and defective experience, I came away merely to avoid the treacheries of London in April. I merely wish to sit by myself in the sun and remember. Therefore, I have a right to expect them to stay away and not interrupt me! *(Looks around. Notices a little alcove, and makes a decision. Calls out.)* Beppo! *Prossimo immediatamente qui!* (Come here immediately!) Beppo!

(BEPPO rushes over. He and MRS. FISHER have an unheard conversation, with MRS. FISHER pointing her cane and gesturing in and out of the house. She then exits into the house. BEPPO nods understanding and moves off into the house.

Lady CAROLINE comes back into the garden, looks to see if she is alone and takes her seat on the garden chaise. She has obviously been crying.

BEPPO begins to set up a small desk and two chairs in the alcove.

A gong is heard from inside the villa. The dining room area is revealed.)

MRS. FISHER *(looking around for her fellow diners)*. Lax! Lax. No manners at all. Francesca! *(FRANCESCA rushes in.)* Servisca prego immediatamente il pranzo. What manners! This is not a hotel and considerations are due! I am surprised at Mrs. Arbuthnot, she at least, had seemed amiable and courteous, whatever else she might be. From the other one, of course, I expect nothing.

(FRANCESCA begins to serve spaghetti. MRS. FISHER stares down at it, not quite knowing how to eat it. The lights in the dining area go down. At the same time ROSE and LOTTY rush into the garden and see Lady CAROLINE.)

ROSE. I am afraid you are not well.
CAROLINE *(without opening her eyes)*. I have a headache.
ROSE. I am so sorry! Do you think hot tea would do you some good?
CAROLINE. No.
LOTTY. I expect what would really be best for her is to be left quiet.
CAROLINE *(opening eyes, startled that LOTTY understands)*. Yes.
ROSE. But I can't bear to think of you with a headache and nothing being done for it. Would a cup of coffee…

LOTTY. I do think that she wants nothing except quiet. *(Pulls ROSE away, smiles at CAROLINE.)*
CAROLINE *(softly after they have left)*. Thank you, Lotty.

(Lights up on dining area after ROSE and LOTTY have entered. ROSE is seated, LOTTY is standing behind her chair, leaning.)

ROSE *(attempting to put long noodles on her fork)*. Lady Caroline has a headache. I can't persuade her to have even a little tea, or some black coffee. Do you know the Italian for aspirin?
MRS. FISHER. The proper remedy for headaches is castor oil.
LOTTY. But she hasn't got a headache.
MRS. FISHER. Carlyle, at one point, suffered terribly from headaches, and he constantly took castor oil as a remedy. He took it, I should say, almost to excess, and called it, I remember, on his interesting way, the oil of sorrow. My father said it colored his whole attitude to life, his whole philosophy. But that was because he took too much. What Lady Caroline wants is one dose and one only. It is a mistake to keep on taking castor oil.
ROSE. Do you know the Italian for it?
MRS. FISHER. Ah, that I am afraid I don't. However, she would know. You can ask her.
LOTTY. But she hasn't got a headache. She only wants to be let alone.
ROSE. Then why would she say she has?
LOTTY. Because she is still trying to be polite. Soon she won't try, when the place has got more into her—she'll really be it…without trying…naturally.

ROSE *(to MRS. FISHER)*. Lotty, you see, has a theory about this place…

MRS. FISHER *(interrupting, turning to LOTTY)*. I am sure I don't know why you should assume Lady Caroline is not telling the truth.

LOTTY. I don't assume. I know.

MRS. FISHER. And pray tell me, how do you know?

LOTTY. I saw inside her.

ROSE *(dropping her head in her hands)*. Oh, dear.

(Lights out in dining area.

Up on garden area.

Lady CAROLINE is in her chair, eyes closed. MRS. FISHER enters from the house, using her cane to move swiftly across the terrace toward her.)

MRS. FISHER. I hear you are not well. I expect the journey has upset you. What you want is a good dose of some simple medication. I shall ask Beppo if there is a chemist in the village who carries castor oil. *(CAROLINE opens her eyes and starts up.)* Ah, I knew you were not asleep. Now, you'll take my advice and not neglect what may very well turn into an illness. We are in Italy, you know, and one has to be careful. You ought, to begin with, to go to bed.

CAROLINE. I never go to bed.

MRS. FISHER. I am sure you'll do what is reasonable. Your mother would wish…have you a mother?

CAROLINE *(smiling)*. Yes. What I want to do here is to come to a conclusion. That's all. It isn't much to want, is it? Just that?

Act II   THE ENCHANTED APRIL   49

MRS. FISHER. I should say that what a young woman like you wants is a husband and children.

CAROLINE. Well, that's one of the things I'm going to consider. But I don't think that would be a conclusion.

MRS. FISHER. And meanwhile, I shouldn't trouble my head if I were you with considering and conclusions. Women's heads weren't made for thinking, I assure you. I should go to bed and get well.

CAROLINE. I am well.

MRS. FISHER. Then why did you send a message that you were ill?

CAROLINE. Wouldn't you prefer coming out and finding me well than coming out and finding me ill?

MRS. FISHER. Well, you're a pretty creature. It's a pity you weren't born fifty years ago. My friends would've liked looking at you.

CAROLINE *(turning away)*. I'm very glad I wasn't. I dislike being looked at.

MRS. FISHER. Absurd. That's what you were made for, young women like you. For what else, pray? And I assure you, if my friends had looked at you, you would've been looked at by some very great people.

CAROLINE. I dislike very great people.

MRS. FISHER. What I dislike is the pose of the modern young woman. It seems to me pitiful, positively pitiful, in its silliness. Sheer silliness, these poses. I have no patience with them. Unable to be or do anything for themselves, your generation tries to achieve a reputation for cleverness by decrying all that was obviously great and obviously good, by praising everything, however obviously bad, that was different. Sheer silliness and obstinacy. *(She turns abruptly and heads toward her sitting area.)*

CAROLINE *(to herself, ruefully)*. That's all right. Even my mother thinks I am peculiar. *(She exits to change for dinner.)*

(Lights up in sitting room area. ROSE and LOTTY are seated. LOTTY is writing a letter. They look up as MRS. FISHER comes into the area.)

ROSE *(to MRS. FISHER)*. Isn't this a delightful place? We have just discovered it.

LOTTY. I'm writing to Mellersh. He'll want to know that I got here safely.

MRS. FISHER. Well!

LOTTY. You don't like us being in here. Why?

MRS. FISHER *(quite indignant)*. I should have thought that you could have seen that it is MY room.

LOTTY. You mean because of the photographs…

MRS. FISHER. And the notepaper…notepaper with MY London address on it. That pen!

LOTTY. …is yours. I'm very sorry! *(Hands it to her.)* It has been writing some very amiable and pleasant things.

ROSE. But why ought we not be here? It's a sitting room.

MRS. FISHER. There is another one. You and your friends cannot sit in two rooms at once, and if I have no wish to disturb you in yours I am unable to see why you should wish to disturb me in mine.

ROSE *(stubbornly)*. But why…?

LOTTY. It's quite natural… *(Intervening.)* …Isn't it, Rose? Soon you'll want us to share. Why you may even get so far as asking me to use your pen if you knew I hadn't got one.

MRS. FISHER. I am an old woman and I need a room to myself. I cannot get about because of my stick. As I cannot get about, I have to sit. Why should I not sit quietly and undisturbed, as I told you in London I intended to? If people are to come in and out all day long, chattering and leaving doors open, you will have broken the agreement, which was that I was to be left quiet!

ROSE. But we haven't the least wish...

LOTTY. We are only too glad for you to have this room if it makes you happy. We didn't know about it, that's all. We wouldn't have come in if we had known, not till you invited us, anyhow. I expect you soon will. *(She drags ROSE out of the area. MRS. FISHER sits at desk forlornly.)*

(Lights up in terrace area.

Down in alcove.)

LOTTY. Poor old thing. Fancy that...on a day like this.

ROSE. She's a very rude old thing.

LOTTY. She'll get over that. I'm sorry we chose her room to go and sit in.

ROSE. It's much the nicest. And it isn't hers.

LOTTY. Oh, but there are lots of other places, and she's such a poor old thing. Let her have the room. Whatever does it matter? I've been thinking about Mellersh.

ROSE. Have you?

LOTTY. I've been a mean dog.

ROSE. A what?

LOTTY. All this coming away and leaving him in that dreary place while I rollick in heaven. He had planned to take me to Italy for Easter himself. Did I tell you?

ROSE. No.

LOTTY. Well, he did. He had never done such a thing in his life before, and I was horrified. Fancy—just as I had planned to come to it myself. Now you see why I say I've been a mean dog. He had planned a holiday in Italy with me, and I had planned a holiday in Italy leaving him at home. I think Mellersh has every reason to be both angry and hurt.

ROSE. Lotty, I am astonished. I shouldn't be sure of that too quickly.

LOTTY. But I am sure of it, and I've written and told him so.

ROSE. But only this morning...

LOTTY. It's all in this. *(Tapping the letter against her hand.)*

ROSE. What? Everything?

LOTTY. You mean about the advertisement and my savings being spent? Oh, no, not yet. But I'll tell him all that when he comes.

ROSE. When he comes?

LOTTY. I've invited him to come and stay with us. *(ROSE stares at her.)* It's the least I could do. Besides, look at this. *(Waves around, indicating garden.)* Disgusting not to share it. I was a mean dog to go off and leave him.

ROSE. But do you think he will come?

LOTTY. Oh, I hope so. Poor lamb.

ROSE. Poor lamb? I need to sit down and catch my breath. Mellersh a poor lamb? The same Mellersh who a few hours ago was a mere shimmer? Mellersh at San Salvatore?

LOTTY *(simply)*. I see him here.

ROSE. I wish I understood you.

LOTTY *(smiling)*. Don't try.

ROSE. But I must. You're my dearest friend. I love you. *(Pause.)* You're so quick. I can't follow your developments. I can't keep touch. It was what happened with Freder... *(She breaks off.)* The whole idea of our coming here was to get away, wasn't it? And now after only a single day of it, you want to write the very people we...

LOTTY. The very people we were getting away from. It's quite true. It seems idiotically illogical. But I'm so happy. I'm so well. I feel so fearfully wholesome. This place makes me feel flooded with love.

ROSE *(a pause)*. And do you think it will have the same effect on Mr. Wilkins?

LOTTY *(laughs joyfully)*. I don't know! I was a stingy beast at home and used to measure and count. I had a queer obsession about justice. As though justice mattered. At home I wouldn't love Mellersh unless he loved me back, exactly as much, absolute fairness. So I've written to him, inviting him to San Salvatore. And I am going to the village to post it. Would you like to come with me?

ROSE *(hesitates)*. I don't think I'll come down to the village today. I think I want to think.

LOTTY. Don't think too long. Write and invite him at once. *(Turns to go.)*

ROSE. Invite whom?

LOTTY *(over her shoulder to ROSE)*. Your husband. *(She exits through the garden path.)*

ROSE. How I wish I could write to my husband and say "Come to me." Lotty can write to Mellersh, she will get her answer and he will come. I can't write to Frederick because I know he will not answer. Well, he might answer. A hurried scribble, showing how bored he was in writing it...thank you so much for your letter. Yes, that would be worse than no answer at all. I remember the letters he wrote in the beginning, the letters so desolate with separation, so aching with love and longing. It would hurt to see my name on an envelope, open it and find "Dear Rose, Thanks for the letter. Glad you're having a good time. Don't hurry back. Say if you want money. Everything going splendidly here. Yours, Frederick" *(Pause.)* No. I wouldn't be able to bear that. *(She exits into the villa.)*

CAROLINE *(entering, dressed for dinner)*. Once again I have the feeling that my life till now has been not only loud but empty. Well, if that is so, if the first twenty-eight years of my life, the best years, have gone by in some meaningless noise, I better stop and take a look around, pause and consider things. I haven't got many sets of twenty-eight years. One more set will see me looking like Mrs. Fisher. Two more... *(She sighs.)* My mother would be very concerned if she could see me now. My father too. I can hear them now. To go away alone is bad...to *think*...worse. *(Sounding like her mother.)* No good can come out of the thinking of a beautiful woman. Thinking is bound to result in hesitations, complications, in unhappiness all around. *(Her own voice.)* Thinking about such things. Such old things. Things nobody ever begins to think about until they are forty. *(She exits into dining area.)*

Act II   THE ENCHANTED APRIL   55

(Dining area lights up. LOTTY, ROSE and MRS. FISHER are already seated.)

LOTTY *(as CAROLINE enters dining area)*. What a beautiful dress!
CAROLINE. What, this old rag? I've had it a hundred years.
MRS. FISHER. You must be very cold in it.
CAROLINE. Who, me? Oh, no.
MRS. FISHER. You mustn't catch a chill you know. There's a great difference when the sun goes down.
CAROLINE. I am quite warm.
MRS. FISHER. You look as though you have nothing at all on underneath.
CAROLINE. I haven't. At least, hardly anything.
MRS. FISHER. How very imprudent, and highly improper.
LOTTY. But there are no men here, so how could it be improper? Have you noticed how difficult it is to be improper without men?
MRS. FISHER. Well, I never!
LOTTY. I've had the most wonderful day.

(CAROLINE takes a huge gulp of her wine.)

MRS. FISHER *(to CAROLINE)*. That is very bad for you.

(CAROLINE takes another gulp.)

LOTTY. I've decided to invite someone to stay with us.
MRS. FISHER *(quite put out)*. Whom do you wish to invite? What is this person's name?
LOTTY. Wilkins.

MRS. FISHER. Wilkins?

LOTTY. Yes.

MRS. FISHER. Your name?

LOTTY. And his.

MRS. FISHER. A relation?

LOTTY. Not blood.

MRS. FISHER. A connection?

LOTTY. A husband. *(Pause.)* You see, we arranged, didn't we, in London that if any of us wanted to we could each invite one guest. So now I am doing it.

MRS. FISHER. I don't remember that.

LOTTY. Oh yes, we did—didn't we, Rose?

CAROLINE. Yes I remember. Only it seemed so incredible that one could ever want to. One's whole idea was to get away from one's friends.

LOTTY. And one's husbands.

CAROLINE. And family affection.

LOTTY. And the want of family affection.

CAROLINE. That wouldn't be so bad. I'd stay with that. It would give one room.

LOTTY. Oh no! That would be dreadful. It's as if one had no clothes on!

CAROLINE. But I like that!

MRS. FISHER. Well really!

CAROLINE. It's a divine feeling getting rid of things.

LOTTY. Oh, but in a bitter wind to have nothing on and know there will never be anything on and you getting colder and colder till at last you die of it—that's what it is like, living with somebody who didn't love one.

CAROLINE. But didn't he?

LOTTY. Mellersh? He showed no signs of it.

CAROLINE. Delicious.

MRS. FISHER. Really!

LOTTY. I didn't think it was at all delicious. I was miserable. And now since I've been here, I simply stare at myself being miserable about Mellersh.

CAROLINE. You mean he wasn't worth it?

MRS. FISHER. Really!

LOTTY. No, I don't. I mean I suddenly got well. And now that I am well I find that I can't sit here and gloat all to myself. I can't be happy shutting him out. I fell like the Blessed Damozel.

CAROLINE. What is the Blessed Damozel?

MRS. FISHER. Really!

CAROLINE. Ought I to know? I don't know any natural history. It sounds like a bird.

MRS. FISHER. It is a poem.

CAROLINE. Oh.

LOTTY. I'll lend it to you.

CAROLINE. No, thank you.

MRS. FISHER. And its author, though perhaps not quite what one would've wished, was frequently at my father's table.

CAROLINE. What a bore for you! That's what my mother is always doing—inviting authors. I hate authors. I wouldn't mind them so much if they didn't write books. *(Turning back to LOTTY.)* Go on about Mellersh.

MRS. FISHER. Really!

LOTTY. All those empty beds…

CAROLINE. What empty beds?

LOTTY. Eight beds and only four people. I want Rose to invite her husband too. You and Mrs. Fisher haven't got husbands, but why not invite some friends for a glorious time?

MRS. FISHER. There is only ONE unoccupied bedroom in this house.

LOTTY. Only one? Then who are in all the others?

MRS. FISHER. We are. We have four bedrooms, Francesca has the fifth, and the sixth is empty.

LOTTY. What a problem.

CAROLINE. What is?

LOTTY. Where to put Mellersh.

CAROLINE. Why, isn't one room enough for him?

LOTTY. Oh, yes, quite! But then there wouldn't be any room left at all—any room for somebody you may wish to invite.

CAROLINE. I shan't want to.

LOTTY *(to MRS. FISHER)*. Or you. Rose, of course, doesn't count. I'm sure she would like sharing her room with her husband. It's written all over her!

MRS. FISHER. Really!

LOTTY. Really what?

MRS. FISHER. Really! Am I to understand that you propose to reserve the one spare room for the exclusive use of your family?

LOTTY. He isn't my own family. He's my husband. You see...

MRS. FISHER. I SEE nothing. At the most I hear, and that, reluctantly.

CAROLINE. I don't see why Mellersh shouldn't have the spare room.

LOTTY. Well, if nobody wants the room, and wouldn't use it anyhow, I shall be very glad if Mellersh may have it.

CAROLINE. Of course, he must have it.

Act II THE ENCHANTED APRIL 59

MRS. FISHER. I have a friend. *(Sudden silence.)* Kate Lumley. Perhaps you know her? I wish to invite her to join me. *(Complete silence.)*

CAROLINE. I'm afraid you're in for it then. Unless he can't come.

LOTTY. I see him here.

MRS. FISHER. Really!

(Lights off on dining area.

Lights up in garden.

The next afternoon.

SERVANTS are seen moving about the garden area, setting up a chair, raking the flowerbeds, etc.

MRS. FISHER appears in her alcove area, restlessly moving about without her cane.

CAROLINE is walking up and down listlessly in the garden.

ROSE sits in another part of the garden, knees tucked up, and arms clasped around them.

Each one speaks without acknowledging the others.)

MRS. FISHER. I have had a curious day and I am a little worried.

ROSE. I have had a curious day. My mind has been quite active, my body quite still.

CAROLINE. How curious. This place has had an almost instantaneous influence on me.

MRS. FISHER. I have not been able to settle on anything and I have done nothing but wander restlessly from my sitting room to the battlements.

ROSE. For years I have taken great care to have no time to think. My scheduled life in the parish prevented time for memories and desires from intruding.

CAROLINE. This place makes me want to sit and think. It acts on me, curiously, like a conscience.

MRS. FISHER. It has been a wasted day. I dislike waste.

ROSE. I feel dejected. How odd to feel so dejected in this place with everything around me making me feel as if I should rejoice.

CAROLINE. But having never thought out anything in my life, I find it quite difficult. Extraordinary how my mind keeps slipping sideways.

MRS. FISHER. Curious that I should be so restless. Very odd that I shouldn't be able to sit still.

ROSE. I sat so still that presently some tiny lizards darted around my feet and some tiny birds flitted in the bushes near me.

CAROLINE. I tried settling myself down to review my past as a preliminary to considering my future and the next thing I know I am thinking about Lotty and Mr. Wilkins.

MRS. FISHER. It would be interesting to talk to someone about it. Not to Kate Lumley, but to a stranger. Kate would only look at me and suggest a cup of tea. How odd. I believe that of all of them, Mrs. Wilkins…Lotty, would understand.

ROSE. What is the good of this with no one here, no one who loved being with one, who belonged to one, to whom one could say "Look, dearest"? That sweet word,

Act II THE ENCHANTED APRIL 61

just to say it to somebody who loved one, would make one happy.

CAROLINE. I hope Mr. Wilkins will not wish to hang about me. Men do. I don't want them to. I would particularly dislike to see the light in Mrs. Wilkins' funny flickering face be blown out. I hope he will be the exception to the dreadful rule. If so, I might like him for it.

(FRANCESCA comes in and serves tea on a table on the patio. One by one the women join the table.

LOTTY comes in last, holding an enormous bouquet of flowers.)

LOTTY *(to ROSE)*. Letter gone?
CAROLINE. What letter?
LOTTY. Asking her husband here.
MRS. FISHER. Another husband. Is there to be no end to them?
LOTTY *(to ROSE)*. Has it?
ROSE. No.
LOTTY. Well, tomorrow then.
MRS. FISHER. Who is your husband?
ROSE. Mr. Arbuthnot.
MRS. FISHER. I mean, of course, what is Mr. Arbuthnot?
ROSE *(quite deliberately)*. My husband.

(CAROLINE laughs delightfully while MRS. FISHER grumbles.

Lights out on the area.

The women exit.

Lights up on archway at back of patio. MELLERSH is having difficulties with the hill he has just climbed and his heavy suitcase. LOTTY is flittering around him being helpful.)

LOTTY. Oh, Mellersh. I am so glad you've come! You must have telegraphed immediately after receiving my letter.

MELLERSH. Lotty, dear, I am not a man to lose time when it comes to business. When I received your letter informing me of the identity of your fellow guests, I perceived that this was an opportunity which may never recur. You are really helping me, my dear. I have it all neatly mapped out in my mind. First, I will have a shave and a bath, put on clean clothes, take a short nap and then I will come to lunch. Then you may introduce me to Lady Caroline.

LOTTY. Oh, Mellersh.

MELLERSH. I have selected the words of my greeting; I went over them with some care. I'll start with some slight expression of my gratification in meeting one of whom I, in common with the whole world, had heard. I'll make a slight reference to her distinguished parents, a sentence or two about her elder brother, Lord Winchcombe, who won his V.C. in the late war in an incident which makes every Englishman's heart beat with pride. And who knows, perhaps the first steps toward what might well be the turning point in my career will have been taken!

LOTTY *(a bit disappointed)*. Of course, Mellersh. *(MELLERSH glances down and notices her disappointment. He*

Act II   THE ENCHANTED APRIL   63

gives her a slight peck on the cheek. She is surprised.)
Oh, Mellersh! *(They exit into the villa.)*

(CAROLINE enters from the back garden, wanders restlessly.

MRS. FISHER enters, notices CAROLINE, hesitates and then walks toward her sitting area.

CAROLINE starts toward MRS. FISHER but changes her mind and goes to recline on the chaise. After a moment, she gets up, restless, and paces in the garden.

Both notice the voices coming from inside the villa—MRS. FISHER with some annoyance, Lady CAROLINE somewhat amused.)

MELLERSH *(offstage to SERVANTS)*. Yes. Yes. Thank you. Lotty, do I give this fellow anything? Which way is the bath?
LOTTY *(offstage, overlapping MELLERSH)*. No, Mellersh, you don't have to give him anything. He lives here. Yes. Of course you may have a bath. It's where you see the crowd.

(Noises of SERVANTS running back and forth.

FRANCESCA's voice and BEPPO's voice heard shouting "Pericoloso."

MELLERSH reassuring them he doesn't need anything.

There is a brief pause. Then an explosion!

MELLERSH runs out onto the terrace with nothing on but a towel wrapped around his waist.)

MELLERSH. That DAMNED bath! *(He turns abruptly to see Lady CAROLINE standing directly behind him.)* Oh, good heavens! I do beg your pardon!

CAROLINE *(holding out her hand)*. How do you do.

MELLERSH *(ever the proper gentleman, even as he is embarrassed)*. I am afraid I used unpardonable language.

CAROLINE. I thought it most appropriate.

MELLERSH. It is Lady Caroline Dester, is it not, to whom I am speaking?

CAROLINE. Yes.

MELLERSH *(attempting to make the most of the situation, covering his embarrassment)*. Allow me to introduce myself. My name is Mellersh Wilkins.

CAROLINE. I thought perhaps it was. *(Sees MRS. FISHER, turns MELLERSH's attention toward her.)* Mrs. Fisher, do let me introduce Mr. Mellersh Wilkins. He has just arrived. *(Turning to MELLERSH.)* This is Mrs. Fisher.

MELLERSH. It is a pleasure to meet a friend of my wife's. *(He holds out his hand in greeting. MRS. FISHER is stunned.)* If you would excuse me, I will go and get dressed now. *(Bowing to each of them.)* Mrs. Fisher. *(A dignified bow.)* Lady Caroline. *(He exits with as much dignity as he can muster.)*

(CAROLINE and MRS. FISHER share a smile and a nod then move back into their areas of the garden. CAROLINE reclines in her sunning chair, a slight smile on her face, more relaxed. MRS. FISHER goes into her sitting

area, starts to write a letter, then puts her pen down and sighs. BEPPO crosses to Lady CAROLINE and offers her a parasol which she accepts graciously. He crosses to LOTTY as she enters and gives her a huge bouquet of freshly picked flowers. He returns to work in the garden. LOTTY puts one flower on MRS. FISHER's table, smiling at MRS. FISHER. She gives a few to CAROLINE who smiles and thanks her. She then goes to BEPPO and has a discussion of the different types of flowers and other garden topics. MELLERSH reenters, fully dressed, bows to MRS. FISHER, who smiles and then exits. Lady CAROLINE waves and exits through the garden.

MELLERSH sees LOTTY and joins her. BEPPO exits.)

LOTTY. Oh, Mellersh! I had expected San Salvatore to take at least two days before it began to work on you, before you got to this stage, but the spell has worked instantly!

MELLERSH *(a bit taken aback but willing to be charmed).* Spell, Lotty? Lady Caroline and Mrs. Fisher were quite gracious after my...moment of introduction. And you, my dear, you are looking quite nice this evening. *(He plays with her hair for an instant, then impulsively kisses her on the cheek.)*

LOTTY. Oh, Mellersh! You have never kissed me like that other than good morning or good night. I am not afraid of you at all!

MELLERSH. Lotty? Whatever do you...

(FRANCESCA storms in and is shaking a pile of papers in LOTTY's face. She speaks loudly and urgently.)

FRANCESCA. *Ho battuto su tutto il portello, persino quello vecchio e non posso trovare chiunque per dirmi come sono supposto pagare queste fatture! Ho bisogno dei soldi di pagare le fatture!* (I have knocked on everyone's door, even the old one, and I cannot find anyone to tell me how I am supposed to pay these bills! I need money to pay the bills!)

LOTTY. Oh, dear. *(Takes the papers.)*

MELLERSH. Whatever does this woman want?

LOTTY. Money.

MELLERSH. Money?

LOTTY. It's the housekeeping bills.

MELLERSH. Well, you have nothing to do with those.

LOTTY. Oh, yes I have. I am so sorry, Mellersh. I have been a brute. I have used my nest egg to pay for a holiday with these women. Mrs. Arbuthnot and I advertised for two companions to join us and that is how Lady Caroline and Mrs. Fisher came to join us. You have every right to be angry I think, but I hope you won't be and forgive me instead.

MELLERSH *(pause. Takes it all in trying to understand. A smile)*. Well, what can be more beneficial than such a holiday?

(MRS. FISHER enters. FRANCESCA stomps over to her.)

LOTTY. Oh, Mellersh, you really are too sweet! Wonderful! *(She throws her arms around him. He hugs her back after a moment, startled but pleased. They wander off to the back corner of the garden.)*

Act II   THE ENCHANTED APRIL   67

FRANCESCA *(to MRS. FISHER, angrily)*. *Chi sta andando pagare le fatture? Devo pagare i miei parenti. A meno che qualcuno mi dia i soldi per pagare queste fatture nessuno mi daranno l'accreditamento per l'alimento della settimana prossima.* (WHO is going to pay the bills? I have to pay my relatives. Unless someone gives me money to pay these bills no one will give me credit for next week's food.)

MRS. FISHER *(looking over the bills)*. I am horrified by the extravagance to which these bills testify!

(FRANCESCA throws her hands up and storms off shouting out in Italian. LOTTY hears this and goes after her. MELLERSH walks toward MRS. FISHER, steps in front of her and tips his hat.)

MELLERSH. May I join you?

MRS. FISHER. I want to find Lady Caroline.

MELLERSH. An agreeable quest. May I assist in the search? *(Holding out his arm, bowing.)* Allow me.

MRS. FISHER *(not yet ready to be charmed)*. I don't know about its being an agreeable quest. She has been letting the bills run up in the most terrible fashion and needs a good scolding.

MELLERSH. Lady Caroline has? What has Lady Caroline to do with the bills here?

MRS. FISHER. The housekeeping was left to her, and as we all share alike it ought to have been a matter of honor with her…

MELLERSH. But—Lady Caroline housekeeping for a party here? A party which includes my wife? My dear lady, you render me speechless. Do you not know she is the daughter of the Droitwhiches...

MRS. FISHER. The Droitwhiches are neither here nor there. Duties undertaken should be performed. I don't intend my money to be squandered for the sake of any Droitwhiches.

(CAROLINE enters and walks toward the garden chaise. MRS. FISHER stomps off toward CAROLINE. MELLERSH hesitates, then follows.)

CAROLINE *(looking up, smiles)*. Hello.

MRS. FISHER. You ought to have told me you were not taking care of the household bills.

CAROLINE. I didn't know you thought I was.

MRS. FISHER. I would like to know what you propose to do for the rest of the time here.

CAROLINE. Nothing.

MRS. FISHER. Nothing! Do you mean to say...

MELLERSH *(intervening)*. If I may be allowed, ladies, to make a suggestion. I would advise you not to spoil a delightful holiday with worries over housekeeping.

MRS. FISHER. Exactly. It is what I intend to avoid.

MELLERSH. Most sensible. Why not, then, allow the cook, an excellent cook by the way, so much a head per diem, and tell her that for this sum she must cater for you, and not only cater but cater as well as ever? One could easily reckon it out. The charges of a moderate hotel, for instance, would do as a basis, halved, or perhaps even quartered.

Act II THE ENCHANTED APRIL

MRS. FISHER. And what about this week that has just passed? The terrible bills of the first week? What about them?

CAROLINE. They shall be my present to San Salvatore. I don't want Lotty to worry about her nest egg being reduced further.

(MELLERSH is taken aback by this remark.)

MRS. FISHER. Really! Of course, if you choose to throw your money about...

MELLERSH. On behalf of my wife, Lady Caroline, may I express all the thanks she would wish to express at this moment. *(Turning to MRS. FISHER, holding out his arm.)* Mrs. Fisher, should we go and find my wife? *(CAROLINE smiles and wanders off.)* I believe it is customary to write a letter of thanks for hospitality. Perhaps you could assist me in helping Lotty word it correctly. You have a delightful knowledge of literature and words, Lotty tells me.

(They exit, passing ROSE who has just come from the house, a letter in her hand.)

ROSE *(watching MELLERSH with MRS. FISHER)*. If Mr. Wilkins can be changed, why not Frederick? How wonderful it would be, how too wonderful if San Salvatore worked on him too. If San Salvatore were able to make them even a little understand each other, even be friends a little. I am beginning to think that my obstinate straitlacedness about his books and my total absorption in good works has been foolish. And perhaps even wrong.

Frederick is my husband and I have frightened him away. I have frightened love away, precious love, and that can't be good. *(She looks down at the letter.)* But once love is frightened away, could it ever come back? *(Looks around garden.)* Yes, it might. Here it might in the atmosphere of Lotty's happiness and San Salvatore. I will mail this letter and when he comes I will try to explain, to ask for something different in our lives for the future.

(ROSE hesitates, looks down at the letter. Then she turns, sadly, back toward the villa and goes slowly in.

She passes MRS. FISHER coming into the garden.)

MRS. FISHER *(entering, moving toward her sitting room, pacing without her walking stick)*. I am so restless. My restlessness has increased this week so much that I might as well not have a sitting room at all, for I can no longer sit. I have had the strangest sensation, as if I were a young tree and the spring has caused the sap to rise in me. I know this feeling. I sometimes had it in childhood in especially swift springs when the lilacs and wisteria seemed to blossom overnight. How worrisome and strange to have this feeling again after fifty years. I feel as if I were going to blossom. How ridiculous! I have heard of old staffs, pieces of mere dried wood, suddenly putting forth fresh leaves, but only in legend. I am not a legend. I know perfectly well what dignity is due and I will have nothing whatsoever to do with blossoming or bursting out in green leaves. How absurd. *(Pause.)* And yet there it is; this feeling that at any moment, I might crop out all green. I wish I could talk to someone who could help me understand. There is no one who would understand except Lotty Wilkins. *(Pause.)* No, that is impossible.

(She sits in her sitting room. Looks around. Alone. She exits after the lights dim in the area.)

MELLERSH *(entering the garden area)*. It is my one aim during my stay at San Salvatore to be a treasure. At all costs the three ladies who are not my wife must like me and trust me. Then, presently when trouble arises in their lives, and in what lives does not trouble arise sooner or later, they will recollect how reliable I am and how sympathetic, and turn to me for advice. Ladies with something on their minds are exactly what I want. Lady Caroline, I judge, has nothing on her mind at this moment, but so much beauty, for I could not but see what was evident, must have its difficulties in the past and she will have more of them before she is done. In the past, I was not at hand. In the future, I hope to be. The behavior of Mrs. Fisher, the next in importance of these ladies from a professional point of view, shows definite promise. I am almost certain Mrs. Fisher has something on her mind. I have been observing her attentively. It is almost certain. With Mrs. Arbuthnot, the third, I have made the least headway. She is so very quiet and retiring. But might not this very retiring nature, the tendency to avoid the others and spend her time alone, indicate that she too was troubled? I will sit and talk with her and encourage her to tell me about herself. *(Pause.)* Lotty has been most charming. She really has all those qualities I credited her with during our courtship. They have only been in abeyance. My early impressions of her are now being endorsed by Lady Caroline Dester, a woman of the world who could not be mistaken on such a subject. Lotty has become that which before marriage what I believed her to be. She is valuable. A man in my profession is always immensely helped by a clever and attractive wife. *(A pause. He absentmindedly touches the cheek she kissed.)* Why had she not been so attractive sooner? *(Pause.)* I think Lotty is quite correct. There is something in San Salvatore that brings out dormant qualities. *(Looks around the garden. Picks a flower.)* I can't remember ever having had a more agreeable holiday. I don't even care what it costs. *(Thinks a moment.)* I will surprise Lotty by presenting her with her nest egg as intact as when she started this holiday. That will be a happy surprise. *(He smiles and exits.)*

(ROSE enters with her letter. She paces in the garden for a moment. She makes a decision and calls for BEPPO. LOTTY enters unseen behind her. When he comes in, ROSE holds out the letter and with gestures indicates that she wishes him to take it to be posted. He bows, understanding, and goes off.)

LOTTY. Now we shall be completely happy!

(CAROLINE and MELLERSH enter with a picnic basket, hats in hand, laughing and heading for the back garden gate. As they join LOTTY, MRS. FISHER enters and walks slowly toward her sitting area. LOTTY notices MRS. FISHER sitting alone.)

LOTTY. Poor old thing. She hasn't got love.
MELLERSH *(scandalized)*. Love? But really, Lotty, at her age…

(CAROLINE giggles.)

LOTTY. Any love.
MELLERSH. And Mrs. Arbuthnot deciding not to come with us?
LOTTY. She wants her husband.
MELLERSH. Ah, very proper.

(CAROLINE turns away, thoughtfully.)

LOTTY. One does.
MELLERSH. Does one? *(He smiles down at her.)*
LOTTY *(beaming up at him)*. Of course. *(She looks back at MRS. FISHER, frowns.)*

(MELLERSH notices LOTTY's concern, looks over, sees MRS. FISHER, then whispers in LOTTY's ear. She smiles up at him gratefully and kisses him on the cheek. She and CAROLINE head out with the basket.

MELLERSH walks over to MRS. FISHER. He gallantly bows, points toward the garden and holds out his arm for MRS. FISHER. She smiles and coyly curtsies to him. They then walk out in the garden, finally sitting on the bench.)

MELLERSH. Now we can sit quite comfortably and enjoy the wonders of nature.

MRS. FISHER. How kind of you to stay and cheer an old woman's solitude.

(BEPPO enters. He looks around the garden, sees MELLERSH and hands him a telegram. He bows and exits.)

MELLERSH. It's for Mrs. Arbuthnot. A pity I do not know where she is. Ought we to open it?

MRS. FISHER. No.

MELLERSH. It may require an immediate answer.

MRS. FISHER. I do not approve of tampering with other people's correspondence.

MELLERSH. Tampering? My dear Mrs. Fisher... *(Sees ROSE enter through the garden.)* Ah, Mrs. Arbuthnot. A telegram has come for you. Beppo looked for you... *(He is startled when ROSE rushes to him and takes the telegram from his hands. Notices ROSE turning white, and staring off after reading the telegram.)* No bad news, I trust?

ROSE *(trying to compose herself)*. Oh, no. On the contrary, I am going to have a visitor. *(She hands the telegram to MELLERSH.)*

MELLERSH *(reading)*. Am passing through on way to Rome. May I pay my respects this afternoon? Thomas Briggs. *(Looks up.)* Who is Thomas Briggs?

ROSE. He is the owner. This is his house. He is very nice. He is coming this afternoon. *(She takes the telegram back from MELLERSH and exits slowly into the villa.)*

MELLERSH *(to MRS. FISHER)*. Shall we assist Mrs. Arbuthnot in preparing for Mr. Briggs' arrival? *(He escorts her into the villa.)*

Act II THE ENCHANTED APRIL 75

(MR. BRIGGS enters from the back of the garden area. He starts toward the villa but then hesitates.)

MR. BRIGGS. An owner of delicacy should not intrude on a tenant. But I have been thinking so much of her since she came to my London townhome. Rose Arbuthnot. Such a pretty name. And such a pretty creature. I was passing so near. It seemed absurd not just to look in and see if she were comfortable. San Salvatore has lately seemed forlorn. It seemed to echo the last time I walked here. I felt lonely here, so lonely that this year I decided to miss the spring here and rent San Salvatore to someone else. It needs a wife. *(Pause.)* I long to see her in my house, to see it as her background, sitting in my chairs, using all the things in my house. Has she seen the portrait of herself on the stairs? I wonder if she likes it.

(He turns to go inside just as FRANCESCA flies out the door toward him yelling vociferously.)

FRANCESCA. *Tutto è nell'ordine. Sto facendo il mio meglio. It's il non mio difetto.* (Everything is in order. I am doing my best. It's not my fault!)
BRIGGS. Of course, Francesca, no one doubts you are doing a good job. *Sia calmo. Tutto è benissimo. Sia calmo! (He looks up to see ROSE coming through the villa doors.)* It really is quite extraordinary.

(FRANCESCA throws up her hands and leaves in disgust.)

ROSE *(looking up, startled)*. Oh. How do you do, Mr. Briggs.

BRIGGS. Would you stand still for just a moment? *(ROSE stops, unsure.)* Yes, quite astonishing. Do you mind taking off your hat?

ROSE *(taking off hat)*. My hat?

BRIGGS. Yes, I thought so. I just wanted to make sure.

ROSE. Have you come to compare me to the original Madonna painting?

BRIGGS. You do see how extraordinarily alike…

ROSE. I didn't know I looked so solemn.

BRIGGS. You don't. Not now. You did a moment ago, quite as solemn. *(Remembering his manners, takes her hand.)* Oh, yes. How do you do.

ROSE. You must let me introduce you to Mrs. Fisher. She is having tea in the top garden.

BRIGGS. Who is Mrs. Fisher?

ROSE. One of the four who are staying in your house. You see, Lotty, I mean Mrs. Wilkins, and I found we could not afford renting San Salvatore by ourselves.

BRIGGS. Oh, I see. I don't want to meet Mrs. Fisher just yet. You have your hat, so you were going for a walk. Mayn't I come too? I'd immensely like being shown around by you. Come and show me all the views.

ROSE. Of course. Though it is your house.

BRIGGS. It isn't. It's yours.

ROSE *(smiling)*. Till Monday week. *(He laughs.)* Why are you laughing?

BRIGGS. It's so like coming home.

ROSE. But it is coming home for you to come home here.

BRIGGS. I mean really like coming home. To one's…family. I never had a family. I'm an orphan.

ROSE *(sympathetic)*. Oh, are you? I hope you've not been one very long. No...I mean I hope you have been one very long. No! I don't know what I mean, except that I'm sorry.

BRIGGS *(laughing)*. Oh, I am used to it. I haven't anybody. No sisters or brothers.

ROSE. You're an only child.

BRIGGS. Yes. And there's something about you that is my idea of...a family. So cozy.

ROSE. You wouldn't think so if you could see my home in Hampstead. *(She suddenly realizes that FREDERICK might avoid their home because it lacked coziness.)*

BRIGGS. I don't believe any place you lived in could be anything but exactly like you.

ROSE. You are not going to pretend San Salvatore is like me.

BRIGGS. I do. Surely you admit it is beautiful?

(ROSE smiles shyly.

BRIGGS holds out his arm for ROSE. They stroll out through the garden.

Dining area lights up. FRANCESCA is setting the table. MRS. FISHER enters followed by ROSE and BRIGGS. She is laughing at something he said.)

MRS. FISHER. My dear boy!

(ROSE is astonished to hear her laugh. She notices MR. BRIGGS smiling at her.)

ROSE. Mr. Briggs? What are you smiling about?
BRIGGS. Perhaps I shall tell you one day.

(He assists MRS. FISHER and ROSE into their chairs. LOTTY and MELLERSH enter.)

LOTTY. Oh! Mr. Briggs! How lovely to see you! Mellersh, this is Mr. Briggs, the owner of San Salvatore. Mr. Briggs, this is my husband, Mellersh Wilkins.

(MELLERSH has been noticing the look BRIGGS is casting on ROSE. He is concerned about the situation, but then pleased that LOTTY introduces him by his full name.)

MRS. FISHER. Mr. Briggs, I am sure you have no thoughts we may not hear.
BRIGGS. I'm sure I would be telling you every one of my secrets in a week.
MRS. FISHER *(laughing)*. You would be telling somebody very safe, then. And in return I daresay I would be telling you mine.
MELLERSH *(teasing and charming)*. Ah no, I must protest. I really must. I have the prior claim. I am the older friend. I have known Mrs. Fisher ten days and you, Mr. Briggs, have not yet known her one. I assert my right to be told her secrets first. *(Everyone laughs.)* That is, *(he bows gallantly to MRS. FISHER)* if you have any, which I beg leave to doubt.

(Everyone laughs again, enjoying the banter.)

MRS. FISHER. Oh haven't I?

(More laughter.)

BRIGGS. Then I shall worm them out!

MRS. FISHER. They won't need much worming out. My difficulty is in keeping them from bursting out!

LOTTY. Mrs. Fisher, you have burst your cocoon!

(She bends over and kisses MRS. FISHER on the cheek. MRS. FISHER is startled at first.)

MRS. FISHER. Good gracious! *(Then she laughs with LOTTY.)* Mr. Briggs, you were telling me that you were on your way to Rome?

BRIGGS. Yes, I was on the train to Rome and I thought I would get out at Mezzago just to look in to make sure you were all comfortable. I plan to continue on tomorrow. I will book a room at the inn.

LOTTY. But how ridiculous! Of course you must stay here. It's your house. *(Turning to MRS. FISHER.)* There's Kate Lumley's room. You wouldn't mind Mr. Briggs having it for one night? *(To BRIGGS, laughing.)* Kate Lumley isn't in it, you know.

MRS. FISHER *(laughing as well)*. No, indeed. Kate Lumley was not in that room, very fortunately, for Kate is a very wide person and that room is excessively narrow. *(Laughter.)* Once in, she would fit so tightly that she would never be able to get out again. *(Laughter.)* It is entirely at your disposal, Mr. Briggs. I hope you will do nothing so absurd as to go to a hotel.

LOTTY. Oh, Mrs. Fisher! *(Hugs her tightly.)*

MRS. FISHER. So you see, my dear boy, you must stay here and gives us all a great deal of pleasure in your company.

MELLERSH *(heartily)*. A great deal indeed!

ROSE *(turning toward him)*. Please do.

BRIGGS. How kind of you all. I'd love to be a guest here. What a new sensation. And with three such...I say, oughtn't I to have a fourth hostess?

LOTTY. Yes, there's Lady Caroline.

BRIGGS. Then hadn't we better find out first if she invites me too.

MELLERSH. The daughter of the Droitwhiches, Briggs, is not likely to be wanting in the proper hospitable impulses.

BRIGGS. The daughter of the Droitwhiches...

(He stops, stunned when CAROLINE steps into the dining area.)

MELLERSH. Ah, Lady Caroline! May I present Mr. Briggs, the owner of San Salvatore.

CAROLINE *(taking his hand)*. How do you do. *(She is dismayed to find he is absolutely smitten with her but she hides it with impeccable manners.)*

MELLERSH *(attempting to smooth over the awkward moment)*. The other ladies have invited Mr. Briggs to spend the night. We only need your seal of approval as his fourth hostess.

CAROLINE. That would be wonderful; however, there is only Kate Lumley's room. I thought your friend was expected any moment, Mrs. Fisher.

MRS. FISHER. No, not at all.

MELLERSH. Quite so. Miss Lumley does not arrive today in any case, Lady Caroline, and Mr. Briggs has, unfortunately if I may say so, to continue his journey tomorrow, so that his staying would in no way interfere with Miss Lumley's movements.

(A pause and then the group laughs remembering the previous conversation.)

CAROLINE *(confused)*. Then of course I join in the invitation. *(She attempts to seat herself but BRIGGS is there to help with her chair.)*

MRS. FISHER. Where are your things, Mr. Briggs?

BRIGGS. My things? Oh, yes—I must fetch them. They're in Mezzago. I'll send Beppo. Oh, I am sorry, I keep forgetting myself. *(Addressing them all, but looking at CAROLINE.)* With your permission, ladies.

MRS. FISHER. Tea first, my dear boy!

(Everyone begins to eat and chat quietly as the lights dim on the dining area.

Early evening. A suggestion of moonlight.

CAROLINE enters the terrace area for some solitude only to find MR. BRIGGS in her part of the garden. She is dismayed. MR. BRIGGS looks up to see her and prevents her from leaving abruptly with a question.)

BRIGGS. I hope that you are quite comfortable here? If you are not, I shall...flay the servants alive!

CAROLINE *(politely)*. I am quite comfortable.

BRIGGS. Your room is quite... *(at a loss)* comfortable?

CAROLINE. Yes. *(She turns to go.)*

BRIGGS. Lady Caroline... *(He wants to be charming but doesn't know what to say.)* Shall I see you at dinner?

CAROLINE. Perhaps. Dinner is at eight. *(She turns to go.)*
BRIGGS. Shall I see you at breakfast?
CAROLINE. I usually eat breakfast in my room.
BRIGGS. Lunch, then? Tea?
CAROLINE. Perhaps, Mr. Briggs. *(She goes into the villa.)*
BRIGGS *(watching her go. He is no longer tongue-tied).* She's gone. The sun has gone out as well and the stars are dark and empty.

(He sits forlornly, alone. MELLERSH enters and notices MR. BRIGGS.)

MELLERSH *(entering, jovially).* Ah, Mr. Briggs. Have you noticed the oleander tree? I have just heard the most charming story from Mrs. Fisher. I believe she heard it from Beppo. You see, a much previous owner of this villa was walking up that hill with his old walking stick and the stick became quite firmly fixed in the mud. After several tries he gave up trying to extricate the stick and left it in the garden path. And presently, how long afterwards no one quite remembers, the stick began to sprout! And it grew into this oleander tree. Marvelous story!

(He throws his arm about BRIGGS' shoulders and takes him off pointing out other sights. BRIGGS goes along politely.

CAROLINE enters, looking around, very relieved to find no one in the garden. She goes to one of the garden seats and sits with a sigh. She looks around, suddenly feeling lonely. She drops her head in her hands. The

Act II THE ENCHANTED APRIL 83

sound of someone struggling up the hill gets her attention. She sees the well-known author of London coming toward her. FREDERICK is struggling up the garden path, out of breath, red faced, and sweating heavily.)

CAROLINE. You! Frederick Arundel! Here? My mother promised faithfully to keep my whereabouts a secret!

FREDERICK *(mopping his brow)*. You must forgive me, Lady Caroline. Your mother told me where you were, and as I happened to be passing through on my way to Rome I thought I would get out at Mezzago and just look in to see how you were.

CAROLINE. But didn't my mother tell you I was having a rest cure?

FREDERICK. Yes, she did. And that's why I waited until this late in the day. I thought you would probably sleep through the day, and wake up in time to be fed.

CAROLINE. But...

FREDERICK. I know. I've got nothing to say in excuse. I couldn't help myself.

CAROLINE *(turning away, speaking to herself)*. This comes of my mother insisting on having authors to lunch, and me being much more amiable in appearance than I truly feel. *(Turning back to FREDERICK.)* Well, you must be fed, before I send you on your way.

FREDERICK. May I truly dine with you. In my traveling clothes?

CAROLINE. Of course. I suppose you've left your things at the train station in Mezzago and you will be going on by the night train?

FREDERICK. Or stay overnight in the hotel in Mezzago and go on by train in the morning. But tell me about yourself. London has been extraordinarily dull and empty. Your mother said you were taking a holiday with people she didn't know. I hope they have been kind to you. You look...well, as if your cure had done everything a cure should.

CAROLINE. They have been very kind. I got them out of an advertisement.

FREDERICK. An advertisement.

CAROLINE. It's a good way, I find, to get friends. I'm fonder of one of these than I have been of anybody for years.

FREDERICK. Really? Who is it?

CAROLINE. You shall guess which of them it is when you see them. Now I must go and dress for dinner. See you then. *(She exits, waving flirtatiously at FREDERICK.)*

FREDERICK. Caroline? *(She is gone. He relaxes his posture and rubs his stomach, sore from trying to hold it in. Looks around.)* What a lovely place. *(Walks around, spies a rosebush. Sighs.)* What am I doing? I used to be happy. When Rose and I were first married, I was happy. Then when we lost the child... *(Walks away from the rosebush.)* It's not in me to be unhappy. Life has so many interests to offer, so many friends, so many successes, so many women, only too willing to help me blot out the altered, petrified, suddenly pious, little wife. She sits at home, won't spend my money, is appalled by my books, she drifts further and further away from me. I have tried to have it out with her. She merely turns that patient stare on me and asks me with patient obstinacy, what I think the things I write and live by look like in the eyes of God. I couldn't help myself. I burst into a loud shriek of laughter and rushed out of the house, away from her pathetic, solemn... *(he pauses, and sighs)* dear little face. How we dreamed together, how we planned, how we laughed. Now I feel old. Without Rose's love...I am old. There is no sense of security. Yes, security. *(Looks off where CAROLINE has just exited.)* With Rose, there was never any need to be ashamed of my figure, to make jokes about myself to forestall other people from laughing at me. With her I needn't be ashamed of getting out of breath going up hills, or how I probably appear to young women. Rose would never have noticed those weaknesses, these changes that getting older has made in me. But... *(sits heavily on the garden bench, mops his brow)* I need to feel young. I need to have a woman to listen to my stories, to treat me as if I were still a charming young man. I don't want to hurt Rose. But I'm lonely. *(His head falls down on his chest and he drifts off to sleep.)*

(ROSE enters slowly, deep in thought. She starts to wander through the garden and then notices someone sitting on the bench. She walks closer and is stunned to see that it is her husband. She walks closer, afraid he will disappear. She reaches out and touches him on the shoulder.)

ROSE *(barely able to whisper)*. Frederick? *(Louder.)* Frederick?

FREDERICK *(wakes up, startled)*. Rose?

ROSE *(throwing herself in his arms)*. Oh, Frederick! You came! I always knew you would come.

FREDERICK *(confused)*. Of course, my dear. *(He is startled when she kisses him.)* Rose?

ROSE *(still holding him)*. When did you start?

FREDERICK. Yesterday morning.
ROSE. Oh, the very instant then.
FREDERICK *(struggling to understand)*. Yes, the very instant.
ROSE. How very quickly my letter got to you. I am so glad!
FREDERICK. Rose? Sweetheart...?
ROSE *(holding his face in her hands)*. Beloved husband. *(She throws herself in his arms again. He holds her tightly.)*
BRIGGS *(entering with MRS. FISHER on his arm)*. Oh...I do beg your pardon!
ROSE. Mr. Briggs. This is my husband, Frederick Arbuthnot. Frederick, this is one of my friends, Mr. Briggs. Mrs. Fisher, this is my husband, Frederick Arbuthnot.
MRS. FISHER *(laughing)*. This must now be the last of the husbands...unless Lady Caroline produces one from up her sleeve. How do you do.

(LOTTY and MELLERSH enter. LOTTY runs over and grabs both of FREDERICK's hands.)

LOTTY. Didn't I tell you, Rose? How wonderful!
MELLERSH. Well sir, here we are.

(General introductions follow. BRIGGS wanders toward the door looking for CAROLINE.)

FREDERICK. What a delightful place this is.
LOTTY. It's a tub of love.

(Everyone laughs.)

MRS. FISHER. Let's go into dinner. We won't wait. Lady Caroline is always late.

(FREDERICK is startled. He had forgotten about CAROLINE.)

LOTTY. Yes, let's all go into dinner.

(She takes FREDERICK by the arm. MELLERSH takes in MRS. FISHER. BRIGGS looks around for Lady CAROLINE, but then ROSE touches him on the shoulder. He turns and offers his arm graciously. She smiles up at him and he relaxes and smiles back. They enter the villa.

Lights up in the dining area.

The diners are trying to arrange the seating. MRS. FISHER goes to the head of the table and allows the others to figure it out.)

FREDERICK. Mrs. Wilkins, aren't you sitting next to your husband?
LOTTY. Yes, I am.
FREDERICK *(jokingly)*. Then by all the rules you shouldn't be sitting next to him!
LOTTY. But I want to. I like sitting next to him. I didn't before I came here. *(MELLERSH takes her hand and kisses it. Everyone is smiling.)* It's this place. It makes one understand. You have no idea what a lot you will understand before you're done here. *(She looks intently at FREDERICK. He casts his eyes down.)*
FREDERICK. I hope so.

(He looks up to see LOTTY still watching him. He casts his eyes down again. ROSE takes his hand and he smiles a little. BRIGGS jumps up, startling everyone. FREDERICK winces. LOTTY notices. CAROLINE enters.)

LOTTY *(quickly)*. CAROLINE! Just fancy how quickly Rose's husband has got here!

CAROLINE *(turning smoothly to FREDERICK)*. And me late on your first evening. I do beg your pardon. How do you do. I am Lady Caroline Dester.

(Lights out in the dining area.

The garden in the brilliant moonlight.

LOTTY and CAROLINE are sitting on the garden bench. ROSE is standing a little away from them looking up at the moon. Presently the men come out of the villa. CAROLINE gets up and crosses away from everyone. FREDERICK crosses immediately to ROSE. MELLERSH and BRIGGS are conversing in the doorway. After a moment, LOTTY crosses to CAROLINE.)

LOTTY *(softly to CAROLINE)*. It's love.
CAROLINE. Yes.
LOTTY. It's a great thing to get on with one's loving. Perhaps you can tell me of anything in the world that works such wonders.
CAROLINE. I can't.
LOTTY. I suppose Rose's husband seems to you just an ordinary, good-natured, middle-aged man. Just a rather red, rather round man. He isn't, you know.
CAROLINE. He isn't?

LOTTY. He isn't. Rose sees through all that. That's mere trimmings. She sees what we can't see because she loves him.

CAROLINE. Always love.

LOTTY. Yes.

CAROLINE. Yes. *(Sarcastically.)* Love works wonders. I have had it applied to me in excess! *(Crying.)* If it had let me alone, if it had at least been moderate and infrequent, I might, might have turned out a quite decent, generous-minded, kind human being. And what am I thanks to this love? I am a spoilt, sour, suspicious spinster. *(She puts her head in her hands and cries.)*

LOTTY. Love, Caroline. Love.

(LOTTY kisses her on the cheek, hugs her affectionately and moves over to MELLERSH. They go into the villa. FREDERICK comes over to CAROLINE.)

FREDERICK. I wanted to thank you.

CAROLINE *(turning away)*. Thank me?

FREDERICK. I adored you before because of your beauty. *(She flinches.)* Now I adore you because, when Mrs. Wilkins blurted out who I was, you behaved exactly as a friend would. I want to kiss your shoes! *(He laughs.)*

CAROLINE *(holding out her hand)*. Won't this do instead?

FREDERICK. You're a wonderful person, Caroline. Thank you for being my friend. *(He kisses her hand and crosses back to ROSE. They exit.)*

CAROLINE *(watching him go)*. I am? *(Pause.)* Everyone is happy. Everyone feels loved. Rose and Frederick, Lotty and Mellersh, even Mrs. Fisher has been touched by it. I am happier now than I have been for ages and ages. Lotty would say that it is San Salvatore working its spell of happiness. *(Notices MR. BRIGGS alone, dejected, in the garden.)* Everyone has something from San Salvatore, even me. Everyone except Mr. Briggs! It seems wrong that the owner of San Salvatore should be the only one not to be happy. If he had never let the villa to Lotty I would never have met her. Never had a friend. *(A sudden decision. She turns and goes quickly to MR. BRIGGS.)* Mr. Briggs! I owe you so much!

BRIGGS. You owe me? But it's I who...

CAROLINE. Please, won't you clear your mind of everything except the truth? You don't owe me anything. Why should you?

BRIGGS. I don't owe you anything?

CAROLINE. Oh for goodness sake. For goodness sake! Don't be humble! Why should you be humble? It's ridiculous of you to be humble. You're worth fifty of me.

(She breaks down crying. BRIGGS is unsure what to do at first. He then takes a handkerchief out and holds it out for her. She takes it from him and blows her nose. He smiles gently. She looks at him, smiles, and then laughs as well.

She sniffles a bit. BRIGGS takes the handkerchief, folds it, and gently wipes away her tears. He then holds his arm out for her. They walk slowly out of the garden.

As they exit, CAROLINE puts her head on his shoulder.

Lights up in MRS. FISHER's sitting room. She is alone.)

MRS. FISHER. My dead friends do not seem worth reading tonight. They always say the same things now; over and over again they say the same things. Nothing new can be gotten out of them. No doubt they are greater than everyone I know. But they have one great disadvantage. They are all dead. I crave the living. I see all the loneliness of old age creeping up on me, the loneliness of having outstayed one's welcome in the world, of only being in it on sufferance, the complete loneliness of being an old, childless woman who has failed to make friends. *(LOTTY and MELLERSH enter quietly.)* It seems that people can only be happy in pairs, any sorts of pairs. Husband and wife, parent and child, brother and sister, even friends can be a pair. And where will the other half of my pair be found?

LOTTY *(bending over to kiss her cheek)*. I believe I am the other half of your pair. I believe it's me, positively me, going to be your friend. I see it.

MRS. FISHER *(smiling)*. Where are the others? *MELLERSH adjusts her back cushion.)* Thank you, my dear boy.

LOTTY. The Roses have gone into the lower garden...I think lovemaking...

MRS. FISHER. The Roses?

LOTTY. The Fredericks if you like. They're completely merged and indistinguishable.

MELLERSH. Why not say the Arbuthnots, my dear.

LOTTY. Very well, Mellersh, the Arbuthnots. The Carolines...

MELLERSH *(startled. Not sure he is pleased)*. The Carolines?

LOTTY. Very well, Mellersh, the Briggses, then. I'm sorry if you don't like it.

MELLERSH. Why they've never set eyes on each other before today!

LOTTY. That's true. But that's why they are able to go ahead. I'm sorry, Mellersh; I see them being the Briggses.

MELLERSH. Very well, Lotty.

MRS. FISHER. April will be over soon.

(She sighs. LOTTY takes her hand and leans her head on MRS. FISHER's shoulder. MELLERSH puts his hand on LOTTY's shoulder. She looks up at him and smiles.

Lights dim on the sitting area.

Lights up on May 1 in the garden. A few petals fall from the oleander tree.

BEPPO crosses the garden carrying many suitcases. Lady CAROLINE enters. She is followed by MR. BRIGGS who takes her hand, kisses it and draws her hand through his arm.)

BRIGGS. Don't be sad, my dear. We will come back.

CAROLINE. I hope so. I hope soon.

(They take one last look at the garden and then exit holding hands. FREDERICK and ROSE enter hand in hand. He kisses her in the garden by the roses. She picks a flower and hands it to him.)

ROSE. For you.

FREDERICK. I prefer you.

Act II THE ENCHANTED APRIL

(ROSE giggles, sounding much younger than before. FREDERICK kisses her and takes her hand. ROSE calls out to LOTTY and MRS. FISHER. Then she and FREDERICK exit. LOTTY enters, spins gaily in the garden. MELLERSH enters with MRS. FISHER. She is walking without her stick.)

MRS. FISHER. I no longer need my walking stick.
MELLERSH. Perhaps you would still allow me to offer my arm?

(MELLERSH tucks her hand in his arm, waves to LOTTY urging her to come along. He and MRS. FISHER exit through the garden gate. LOTTY spins around one last time and ends up by the oleander tree. As she reaches up to the branches, colorful petals begin to fall around her. MELLERSH comes back into the garden, sees her there, and comes up to her.)

MELLERSH. Lotty, my dear?
LOTTY. Oh, Mellersh. I am so happy.

(He takes her face in his hands and kisses her gently. Then he pulls her into his arms and kisses her quite thoroughly. Finally, he takes her hand and walks with her out of the garden. The petals continue to fall.)

CURTAIN

EXPANDED CHARACTER DESCRIPTIONS:

- LOTTY WILKINS – Lotty has an overwhelming bubbly and impulsive personality. She blurts out exactly what she is thinking, although others may not completely understand what it is she is trying to say and she almost always immediately regrets saying it. She is free spirited and almost childlike but extremely shy, loving and kind.

- ROSE ARBUTHNOT – Rose is struggling with her relationship with her husband after the loss of their child early in the marriage. Her porcelain Madonna-like features give her an air of fragility but she is determined to live a life of purpose, helping the poor, working at her church. Her peaceful and calm demeanor hides a deep sadness.

- MRS. FISHER – Mrs. Fisher is a widow living alone. Although she has money, she prefers to live in the house her father left her, full of the memories of famous people she knew as a child. Her home is full of pictures of authors and poets. She despises the frivolity of the postwar modern generation and has no time for silliness or people with a lack of decorum.

- LADY CAROLINE DESTER – Caroline is the beautiful and pampered daughter of the Droitwhich family and spends her time flitting from party to party. She has all the training and manners of a well-bred society lady but these mask the terrible sadness and pain inside. The man she loved and would have married was killed in the war. Her beauty gives the impression of being calm and cool even when she is fuming on the inside, and this frustrates her.

MELLERSH WILKINS – Mellersh is an intelligent, precisely mannered accountant, the complete opposite of his wife, Lotty. He thinks out everything he wishes to say and plans every move. He cares deeply about things but feels he must plan his life precisely to be happy. He is frustrated by his wife's impulsive, child-like behavior, wishing she would grow up, settle down and live out his well-planned life. He loves his wife but he doesn't understand her.

FREDERICK ARBUTHNOT – Frederick worked as a civil servant until he began his successful career as an author of racy romantic novels. He is deeply in love with his wife, but since the death of their child, he has retreated from her overwhelming sadness. He is hurt that she criticizes his novels as "sinful." He misses his youth and wants to be seen as an attractive, dashing man.

MR. BRIGGS – Mr. Briggs, a bachelor, is shy, intelligent, and lonely. He decides to rent San Salvatore because he can no longer visit there without feeling his loneliness.

FRANCESCA – Francesca is the overworked housekeeper at San Salvatore. She is volatile, stubborn, and fed up with the crazy English tourists visiting here.

BEPPO – Beppo is the excitable, happy servant. He does all the gardening, heavy labor and carriage driving for San Salvatore's guests.

NOTES